Summer on the Lakes

S.M. Fuller

Contents

SUMMER ON THE LAKES. 7
TO A FRIEND. 8
CHAPTER I. 9
CHAPTER II THE LAKES. 16
CHAPTER III. 34
CHAPTER IV. CHICAGO AGAIN. 53
CHAPTER V. WISCONSIN. 81
CHAPTER VI. MACKINAW. 121
CHAPTER VII. SAULT ST. MARIE. 166

SUMMER ON THE LAKES

BY
S.M. Fuller

SUMMER ON THE LAKES.

Summer days of busy leisure,
Long summer days of dear-bought pleasure,
You have done your teaching well;
Had the scholar means to tell
How grew the vine of bitter-sweet,
What made the path for truant feet,
Winter nights would quickly pass,
Gazing on the magic glass
O'er which the new-world shadows pass;
But, in fault of wizard spell,
Moderns their tale can only tell
In dull words, with a poor reed
Breaking at each time of need.
But those to whom a hint suffices
Mottoes find for all devices,
See the knights behind their shields,
Through dried grasses, blooming fields.

TO A FRIEND.

Some dried grass-tufts from the wide flowery plain,
A muscle shell from the lone fairy shore,
Some antlers from tall woods which never more
To the wild deer a safe retreat can yield,
An eagle's feather which adorned a Brave,
Well-nigh the last of his despairing band,
For such slight gifts wilt thou extend thy hand
When weary hours a brief refreshment crave?
I give you what I can, not what I would,
If my small drinking-cup would hold a flood,
As Scandinavia sung those must contain
With which the giants gods may entertain;
In our dwarf day we drain few drops, and soon must thirst again.

CHAPTER I.

Niagara, June 10, 1843.

Since you are to share with me such foot-notes as may be made on the pages of my life during this summer's wanderings, I should not be quite silent as to this magnificent prologue to the, as yet, unknown drama. Yet I, like others, have little to say where the spectacle is, for once, great enough to fill the whole life, and supersede thought, giving us only its own presence. "It is good to be here," is the best as the simplest expression that occurs to the mind.

We have been here eight days, and I am quite willing to go away. So great a sight soon satisfies, making us content with itself, and with what is less than itself. Our desires, once realized, haunt us again less readily. Having "lived one day" we would depart, and become worthy to live another.

We have not been fortunate in weather, for there cannot be too much, or too warm sunlight for this scene, and the skies have been lowering, with cold, unkind winds. My nerves, too much braced up by such an atmosphere, do not well bear the continual stress of sight and sound. For here there is no escape from the weight of a perpetual creation; all other forms and motions come and go, the tide rises and recedes, the wind, at its mightiest, moves in gales and gusts, but here is really an incessant, an indefatigable motion. Awake or asleep, there is no escape, still this rushing round you and through you. It is in this way I have most felt the grandeur--somewhat eternal, if not infinite.

At times a secondary music rises; the cataract seems to seize its own rhythm and sing it over again, so that the ear and soul are roused by a double vibration. This is some effect of the wind, causing echoes to the thundering anthem. It is very sublime, giving the effect of a spiritual repetition through all the spheres.

When I first came I felt nothing but a quiet satisfaction. I found that drawings, the panorama, &c. had given me a clear notion of the position and proportions of all objects here; I knew where to look for everything, and everything looked as I thought it would.

Long ago, I was looking from a hill-side with a friend at one of the finest sunsets that ever enriched this world. A little cow-boy, trudging along, wondered what we could be gazing at. After spying about some time, he found it could only be the sunset, and looking, too, a moment, he said approvingly "that sun looks well enough;" a speech worthy of Shakspeare's Cloten, or the infant Mercury, up to everything from the cradle, as you please to take it.

Even such a familiarity, worthy of Jonathan, our national hero, in a prince's palace, or "stumping" as he boasts to have done, "up the Vatican stairs, into the Pope's presence, in my old boots," I felt here; it looks really ***well enough***, I felt, and was inclined, as you suggested, to give my approbation as to the one object in the world that would not disappoint.

But all great expression, which, on a superficial survey, seems so easy as well as so simple, furnishes, after a while, to the faithful observer its own standard by which to appreciate it. Daily these proportions widened and towered more and more upon my sight, and I got, at last, a proper foreground for these sublime distances. Before coming away, I think I really saw the full wonder of the scene. After awhile it so drew me into itself as to inspire an undefined dread, such as I never knew before, such as may be felt when death is about to usher us into a new existence. The perpetual trampling of the waters seized my senses. I felt that no other sound, however near, could be heard, and would start and look behind me for a foe. I realized the identity of that mood of nature in which these waters were poured down with such absorbing force, with that in which the Indian was shaped on the same soil. For continually upon my mind came, unsought and unwelcome, images, such as never haunted it before, of naked savages stealing behind me with uplifted tomahawks; again and again this illusion recurred, and even after I had thought it over, and tried to shake it off, I could not help starting and looking behind me.

As picture, the Falls can only be seen from the British side. There they are seen in their veils, and at sufficient distance to appreciate the magical effects of these, and the light and shade. From the boat, as you cross, the effects and contrasts are more melodramatic. On the road back from the whirlpool, we saw them as a reduced picture with delight. But what I liked best was to sit on Table Rock, close to the great fall. There all power of observing details, all separate consciousness, was quite lost.

Once, just as I had seated myself there, a man came to take his first look. He walked close up to the fall, and, after looking at it a moment, with an air as if thinking how he could best appropriate it to his own use, he spat into it.

This trait seemed wholly worthy of an age whose love of ***utility*** is such that the Prince Puckler Muskau suggests the probability of men coming to put the bodies of their dead parents in the fields to fertilize them, and of a country such as Dickens has described; but these will not, I hope, be seen on the historic page to be truly the age or truly the America. A little leaven is leavening the whole mass for other bread.

The whirlpool I like very much. It is seen to advantage after the great falls; it is so sternly solemn. The river cannot look more imperturbable, almost sullen in its marble green, than it does just below the great fall; but the slight circles that mark the hidden vortex, seem to whisper mysteries the thundering voice above could not proclaim,--a meaning as untold as ever.

It is fearful, too, to know, as you look, that whatever has been swallowed by the cataract, is like to rise suddenly to light here, whether uprooted tree, or body of man or bird.

The rapids enchanted me far beyond what I expected; they are so swift that they cease to seem so; you can think only of their beauty. The fountain beyond the Moss Islands, I discovered for myself, and thought it for some time an accidental beauty which it would not do to leave, lest I might never see it again. After I found it permanent, I returned many times to watch the play of its crest. In the little waterfall beyond, nature seems, as she often does, to have made a study for some larger design. She delights in this,--a sketch within a sketch, a dream within a dream. Wherever we see it, the lines of the great buttress in the fragment of stone, the hues of the waterfall, copied in the flowers that star its bordering mosses, we are delighted; for all the lineaments become fluent, and we mould the scene in congenial thought with its genius.

People complain of the buildings at Niagara, and fear to see it further deformed. I cannot sympathize with such an apprehension: the spectacle is capable to swallow up all such objects; they are not seen in the great whole, more than an earthworm in a wide field.

The beautiful wood on Goat Island is full of flowers; many of the fairest love to do homage here. The Wake Robin and May Apple are in bloom now; the former, white, pink, green, purple, copying the rainbow of the fall, and fit to make a garland for its presiding deity when he walks the land, for they are of imperial size, and shaped like stones for a diadem. Of the May Apple, I did not raise one green tent without finding a flower beneath.

And now farewell, Niagara. I have seen thee, and I think all who come here must in some sort see thee; thou art not to be got rid of as easily as the stars. I will be here again beneath some flooding July moon and sun. Owing to the absence of light, I have seen the rainbow only two or three times by day; the lunar bow not at all. However, the imperial presence needs not its crown, though illustrated by it.

General Porter and Jack Downing were not unsuitable figures here. The former heroically planted the bridges by which we cross to Goat Island, and the Wake-Robin-crowned genius has punished his temerity with deafness, which must, I think, have come upon him when he sank the first stone in the rapids. Jack seemed an acute and entertaining representative of Jonathan, come to look at his great water-privilege. He told us all about the Americanisms of the spectacle; that is to say, the battles that have been fought here. It seems strange that men could fight in such a place; but no temple can still the personal griefs and strifes in the breasts of its visiters.

No less strange is the fact that, in this neighborhood, an eagle should be chained for a plaything. When a child, I used often to stand at a window from which I could see an eagle chained in the balcony of a museum. The people used to poke at it with sticks, and my childish heart would swell with indignation as I saw their insults, and the mien with which they were borne by the monarch-bird. Its eye was dull, and its plumage soiled and shabby, yet, in its form and attitude, all the king was visible, though sorrowful and dethroned. I never saw another of the family till, when passing through the Notch of the White Mountains, at that moment striding before us in all the panoply of sunset, the driver shouted, "Look there!" and following with our eyes his upward-pointing finger, we saw, soaring slow in majestic poise above the highest summit, the bird of Jove. It was a glorious sight, yet I know not that I felt more on seeing the bird in all its natural freedom and royalty, than when, imprisoned and insulted, he had filled my early thoughts with the Byronic "silent rages" of misanthropy.

Now, again, I saw him a captive, and addressed by the vulgar with the language they seem to find most appropriate to such occasions--that of thrusts and blows. Silently, his head averted, he ignored their existence, as Plotinus or Sophocles might that of a modern reviewer. Probably, he listened to the voice of the cataract, and felt that congenial powers flowed free, and was consoled, though his own wing was broken.

The story of the Recluse of Niagara interested me a little. It is wonderful that men do not oftener attach their lives to localities of great beauty--that, when once deeply penetrated, they will let themselves so easily be borne away by the general stream of things, to live any where and any how. But there is something ludicrous in being the hermit of a show-place, unlike St. Francis in his mountain-bed, where none but the stars and rising sun ever saw him.

There is also a "guide to the falls," who wears his title labeled on his hat; otherwise, indeed, one might as soon think of asking for a gentleman usher to point out the moon. Yet why should we wonder at such, either, when we have Commentaries on Shakspeare, and Harmonics of the Gospels?

And now you have the little all I have to write. Can it interest you? To one who has enjoyed the full life of any scene, of any hour, what thoughts can be recorded about it, seem like the commas and semicolons in the paragraph, mere stops. Yet I suppose it is not so to the absent. At least, I have read things written about Niagara, music, and the like, that interested *me*. Once I was moved by Mr. Greenwood's remark, that he could not realize this marvel till, opening his eyes the next morning after he had seen it, his doubt as to the possibility of its being still there, taught him what he had experienced. I remember this now with pleasure, though, or because, it is exactly the opposite to what I myself felt. For all greatness affects different minds, each in "its own particular kind," and the variations of testimony mark the truth of feeling.

I will add a brief narrative of the experience of another here, as being much better than anything I could write, because more simple and individual.

"Now that I have left this 'Earth-wonder,' and the emotions it excited are past, it seems not so much like profanation to analyze my feelings, to recall minutely and accurately the effect of this manifestation of the Eternal. But one should go to such a scene prepared to yield entirely to its influences, to forget one's little self and one's little mind. To see a miserable worm creep to the brink of this falling world of waters, and watch the trembling of its own petty bosom, and fancy that this is made alone, to act upon him excites--derision?--No,--pity."

As I rode up to the neighborhood of the falls, a solemn awe imperceptibly stole over me, and the deep sound of the ever-hurrying rapids prepared my mind for the lofty emotions to be experienced. When I reached the hotel, I felt a strange indifference about seeing the aspiration of my life's hopes. I lounged about the rooms, read the stage bills upon the walls, looked over the register, and, finding the name of an acquaintance, sent to see if he was still there. What this hesitation arose from, I know not; perhaps it was a feeling of my unworthiness to enter this temple which nature has erected to its God.

At last, slowly and thoughtfully I walked down to the bridge leading to Goat Island, and when I stood upon this frail support, and saw a quarter of a mile of tumbling, rushing rapids, and heard their everlasting roar, my emotions overpowered me, a choking sensation rose to my throat, a thrill rushed through my veins, "my blood ran rippling to my finger's ends." This was the climax of the effect which the falls produced upon me--neither the American nor the British fall moved me as did these rapids. For the magnificence, the sublimity of the latter I was prepared by descriptions and by paintings. When I arrived in sight of them I merely felt, "ah, yes, here is the fall, just as I have seen it in picture." When I arrived at the terrapin bridge, I expected to be overwhelmed, to retire trembling from this giddy eminence, and gaze with unlimited wonder and awe upon the immense mass rolling on and on, but, somehow or other, I thought only of comparing the effect on my mind with what I had read and heard. I looked for a short time, and then with almost a feeling of disappointment, turned to go to the other points of view to see if I was not mistaken in not feeling any surpassing emotion at this sight. But from the foot of Biddle's stairs, and the middle of the river, and from below the table rock, it was still "barren, barren all." And, provoked with my stupidity in feeling most moved in the wrong place, I turned away to the hotel, determined to set off for Buffalo that afternoon. But the stage did not go, and, after nightfall, as there was a splendid moon, I went down to the bridge, and leaned over the parapet, where the boiling rapids came down in their might. It was grand, and it was also gorgeous; the yellow rays of the moon made the broken waves appear like auburn tresses twining around the black rocks. But they did not inspire me as before. I felt a foreboding of a mightier emotion to rise up and swallow all others, and I passed on to the terrapin bridge. Everything was changed, the misty apparition had taken off its many-colored crown which it had worn by day, and a bow of silvery white spanned its summit. The moonlight gave a poetical indefiniteness to the distant parts of the waters, and while the rapids were glancing in her beams, the river below the falls was black as night, save where the reflection of the sky gave it the appearance of a shield of blued steel. No gaping tourists loitered, eyeing with their glasses, or sketching on cards the hoary locks of the ancient river god. All tended to harmonize with the natural grandeur of the scene. I gazed long. I saw how here mutability and unchangeableness were united. I surveyed the conspiring waters rushing against the rocky ledge to overthrow it at one mad plunge, till, like toppling ambition, o'erleaping themselves, they fall on t'other side, expanding into foam ere they reach the deep channel where they creep submissively away.

Then arose in my breast a genuine admiration, and a humble adoration of the Being who was the architect of this and of all. Happy were the first discoverers of Niagara, those who could come unawares upon this view and upon that, whose feelings were entirely their own. With what gusto does Father Hennepin describe "this great downfall of water," "this vast and prodigious cadence of water, which falls down after a surprising and astonishing manner, insomuch that the universe does not afford its parallel. 'Tis true Italy and Swedeland boast of some such things, but we may well say that they be sorry patterns when compared with this of which we do now speak."

CHAPTER II.
THE LAKES.

SCENE, STEAMBOAT.--About to leave Buffalo--Baggage coming on board--Passengers bustling for their berths--Little boys persecuting everybody with their newspapers and pamphlets--J., S. and M. huddled up in a forlorn corner, behind a large trunk--A heavy rain falling.

M. Water, water everywhere. After Niagara one would like a dry strip of existence. And at any rate it is quite enough for me to have it under foot without having it over head in this way.

J. Ah, do not abuse the gentle element. It is hardly possible to have too much of it, and indeed, if I were obliged to choose amid the four, it would be the one in which I could bear confinement best.

S. You would make a pretty Undine, to be sure!

J. Nay, I only offered myself as a Triton, a boisterous Triton of the sounding shell ... You; M. I suppose, would be a salamander, rather.

M. No! that is too equivocal a position, whether in modern mythology, or Hoffman's tales. I should choose to be a gnome.

J. That choice savors of the pride that apes humility.

M. By no means; the gnomes are the most important of all the elemental tribes. Is it not they who make the money?

J. And are accordingly a dark, mean, scoffing,--

M. You talk as if you had always lived in that wild unprofitable element you are so fond of, where all things glitter, and nothing is gold; all show and no substance. My people work in the secret, and their works praise them in the open light; they remain in the dark because only there such marvels could be bred. You call them mean. They do not spend their energies on their own growth, or their own play, but to feed the veins of mother earth with permanent splendors, very different from what she shows on the surface.

Think of passing a life, not merely in heaping together, but making gold. Of all dreams, that of the alchymist is the most poetical, for he looked at the finest symbol. Gold, says one of our friends, is the hidden light of the earth, it crowns the mineral, as wine the vegetable order, being the last expression of vital energy.

J. Have you paid for your passage?

M. Yes! and in gold, not in shells or pebbles.

J. No really wise gnome would scoff at the water, the beautiful water. "The spirit of man is like the water."

S. Yes, and like the air and fire, no less.

J. Yes, but not like the earth, this low-minded creature's chosen dwelling.

M. The earth is spirit made fruitful,--life. And its heart-beats are told in gold and wine.

J. Oh! it is shocking to hear such sentiments in these times. I thought that Bacchic energy of yours was long since repressed.

M. No! I have only learned to mix water with my wine, and stamp upon my gold the heads of kings, or the hieroglyphics of worship. But since I have learnt to mix with water, let's hear what you have to say in praise of your favorite.

J. From water Venus was born, what more would you have? It is the mother of Beauty, the girdle of earth, and the marriage of nations.

S. Without any of that high-flown poetry, it is enough, I think, that it is the great artist, turning all objects that approach it to picture.

J. True, no object that touches it, whether it be the cart that ploughs the wave for sea-weed, or the boat or plank that rides upon it, but is brought at once from the demesne of coarse utilities into that of picture. All trades, all callings, become picturesque by the water's side, or on the water. The soil, the slovenliness is washed out of every calling by its touch. All river-crafts, sea-crafts, are picturesque, are poetical. Their very slang is poetry.

M. The reasons for that are complex.

J. The reason is, that there can be no plodding, groping words and motions, on my water as there are on your earth. There is no time, no chance for them where all moves so rapidly, though so smoothly, everything connected with water must be like itself, forcible, but clear. That is why sea-slang is so poetical; there is a word for everything and every act, and a thing and an act for every word. Seamen must speak quick and bold, but also with utmost precision. They cannot reef and brace other than in a Homeric dialect--therefore,--(Steamboat bell rings.) But I must say a quick good-by.

M. What, going, going back to earth after all this talk upon the other side. Well, that is nowise Homeric, but truly modern.

J. is borne off without time for any reply, but a laugh--at himself, of course.

S. and M. retire to their state-rooms to forget the wet, the chill and steamboat smell in their just-bought new world of novels.

Next day, when we stopped at Cleveland, the storm was just clearing up; ascending the bluff, we had one of the finest views of the lake that could have been wished. The varying depths of these lakes give to their surface a great variety of coloring, and beneath this wild sky and changeful lights, the waters presented kaleidoscopic varieties of hues, rich, but mournful. I admire these bluffs of red, crumbling earth. Here land and water meet under very different auspices from those of the rock-bound coast to which I have been accustomed. There they meet tenderly to challenge, and proudly to refuse, though not in fact repel. But here they meet to mingle, are always rushing together, and changing places; a new creation takes place beneath the eye.

The weather grew gradually clearer, but not bright; yet we could see the shore and appreciate the extent of these noble waters.

Coming up the river St. Clair, we saw Indians for the first time. They were camped out on the bank. It was twilight, and their blanketed forms, in listless groups or stealing along the bank, with a lounge and a stride so different in its wildness from the rudeness of the white settler, gave me the first feeling that I really approached the West.

The people on the boat were almost all New Englanders, seeking their fortunes. They had brought with them their habits of calculation, their cautious manners, their love of polemics. It grieved me to hear these immigrants who were to be the fathers of a new race, all, from the old man down to the little girl, talking not of what they should do, but of what they should get in the new scene. It was to them a prospect, not of the unfolding nobler energies, but of more ease, and larger accumulation. It wearied me, too, to hear Trinity and Unity discussed in the poor, narrow doctrinal way on these free waters; but that will soon cease, there is not time for this clash of opinions in the West, where the clash of material interests is so noisy. They will need the spirit of religion more than ever to guide them, but will find less time than before for its doctrine. This change was to me, who am tired of the war of words on these subjects, and believe it only sows the wind to reap the whirlwind, refreshing, but I argue nothing from it; there is nothing real in the freedom of thought at the West, it is from the position of men's lives, not the state of their minds. So soon as they have time, unless they grow better meanwhile, they will cavil and criticise, and judge other men by their own standard, and outrage the law of love every way, just as they do with us.

We reached Mackinaw the evening of the third day, but, to my great disappointment, it was too late and too rainy to go ashore. The beauty of the island, though seen under the most unfavorable circumstances, did not disappoint my expectations. But I shall see it to more purpose on my return.

As the day has passed dully, a cold rain preventing us from keeping out in the air, my thoughts have been dwelling on a story told when we were off Detroit, this morning, by a fellow passenger, and whose moral beauty touched me profoundly.

Some years ago, said Mrs. L., my father and mother stopped to dine at Detroit. A short time before dinner my father met in the hall Captain P., a friend of his youthful days. He had loved P. extremely, as did many who knew him, and had not been surprised to hear of the distinction and popular esteem which his wide knowledge, talents, and noble temper commanded, as he went onward in the world. P. was every way fitted to succeed; his aims were high, but not too high for his powers, suggested by an instinct of his own capacities, not by an ideal standard drawn from culture. Though steadfast in his course, it was not to overrun others, his wise self-possession was no less for them than himself. He was thoroughly the gentleman, gentle because manly, and was a striking instance that where there is strength for sincere courtesy, there is no need of other adaptation to the character of others, to make one's way freely and gracefully through the crowd.

My father was delighted to see him, and after a short parley in the hall--"We will dine together," he cried, "then we shall have time to tell all our stories."

P. hesitated a moment, then said, "My wife is with me."

"And mine with me," said my father, "that's well; they, too, will have an opportunity of getting acquainted and can entertain one another, if they get tired of our college stories."

P. acquiesced, with a grave bow, and shortly after they all met in the dining-room. My father was much surprised at the appearance of Mrs. P. He had heard that his friend married abroad, but nothing further, and he was not prepared to see the calm, dignified P. with a woman on his arm, still handsome, indeed, but whose coarse and imperious expression showed as low habits of mind as her exaggerated dress and gesture did of education. Nor could there be a greater contrast to my mother, who, though understanding her claims and place with the certainty of a lady, was soft and retiring in an uncommon degree.

However, there was no time to wonder or fancy; they sat down, and P. engaged in conversation, without much vivacity, but with his usual ease. The first quarter of an hour passed well enough. But soon it was observable that Mrs. P. was drinking glass after glass of wine, to an extent few gentlemen did, even then, and soon that she was actually excited by it. Before this, her manner had been brusque, if not contemptuous towards her new acquaintance; now it became, towards my mother especially, quite rude. Presently she took up some slight remark made by my mother, which, though it did not naturally mean anything of the sort, could be twisted into some reflection upon England, and made it a handle, first of vulgar sarcasm, and then, upon my mother's defending herself with some surprise and gentle dignity, hurled upon her a volley of abuse, beyond Billingsgate.

My mother, confounded, feeling scenes and ideas presented to her mind equally new and painful, sat trembling; she knew not what to do, tears rushed into her eyes. My father, no less distressed, yet unwilling to outrage the feelings of his friend by doing or saying what his indignation prompted, turned an appealing look on P.

Never, as he often said, was the painful expression of that sight effaced from his mind. It haunted his dreams and disturbed his waking thoughts. P. sat with his head bent forward, and his eyes cast down, pale, but calm, with a fixed expression, not merely of patient wo, but of patient shame, which it would not have been thought possible for that, noble countenance to wear, "yet," said my father, "it became him. At other times he was handsome, but then beautiful, though of a beauty saddened and abashed. For a spiritual light borrowed from the worldly perfection of his mien that illustration by contrast, which the penitence of the Magdalen does from the glowing earthliness of her charms."

Seeing that he preserved silence, while Mrs. P. grew still more exasperated, my father rose and led his wife to her own room. Half an hour had passed, in painful and wondering surmises, when a gentle knock was heard at the door, and P. entered equipped for a journey. "We are just going," he said, and holding out his hand, but without looking at them, "Forgive."

They each took his hand, and silently pressed it, then he went without a word more.

Some time passed and they heard now and then of P., as he passed from one army station to another, with his uncongenial companion, who became, it was said, constantly more degraded. Whoever mentioned having seen them, wondered at the chance which had yoked him to such a woman, but yet more at the silent fortitude with which he bore it. Many blamed him for enduring it, apparently without efforts to check her; others answered that he had probably made such at an earlier period, and finding them unavailing, had resigned himself to despair, and was too delicate to meet the scandal that, with such a resistance as such a woman could offer, must attend a formal separation.

But my father, who was not in such haste to come to conclusions, and substitute some plausible explanation for the truth, found something in the look of P. at that trying moment to which none of these explanations offered a key. There was in it, he felt, a fortitude, but not the fortitude of the hero, a religious submission, above the penitent, if not enkindled with the enthusiasm of the martyr.

I have said that my father, was not one of those who are ready to substitute specious explanations for truth, and those who are thus abstinent rarely lay their hand on a thread without making it a clue. Such an one, like the dexterous weaver, lets not one color go, till he finds that which matches it in the pattern; he keeps on weaving, but chooses his shades, and my father found at last what he wanted to make out the pattern for himself. He met a lady who had been intimate with both himself and P. in early days, and finding she had seen the latter abroad, asked if she knew the circumstances of the marriage. "The circumstances of the act I know," she said, "which sealed the misery of our friend, though as much in the dark as any one about the motives that led to it."

We were quite intimate with P. in London, and he was our most delightful companion. He was then in the full flower of the varied accomplishments, which set off his fine manners and dignified character, joined, towards those he loved, with a certain soft willingness which gives the desirable chivalry to a man. None was more clear of choice where his personal affections were not touched, but where they were, it cost him pain to say no, on the slightest occasion. I have thought this must have had some connexion with the mystery of his misfortunes.

One day he called on me, and, without any preface, asked if I would be present next day at his marriage. I was so surprised, and so unpleasantly surprised, that I did not at first answer a word. We had been on terms so familiar, that I thought I knew all about him, yet had never dreamed of his having an attachment, and, though I had never inquired on the subject, yet this reserve, where perfect openness had been supposed, and really, on my side, existed, seemed to me a kind of treachery. Then it is never pleasant to know that a heart, on which we have some claim, is to be given to another. We cannot tell how it will affect our own relations with a person; it may strengthen or it may swallow up other affections; the crisis is hazardous, and our first thought, on such an occasion, is too often for ourselves, at least, mine was. Seeing me silent, he repeated his question.

To whom, said I, are you to be married?

That, he replied, I cannot tell you. He was a moment silent, then continued with an impassive look of cold self-possession, that affected me with strange sadness.

"The name of the person you will hear, of course, at the time, but more I cannot tell you. I need, however, the presence, not only of legal, but of respectable and friendly witnesses. I have hoped you and your husband would do me this kindness. Will you?"

Something in his manner made it impossible to refuse. I answered before I knew I was going to speak, "We will," and he left me.

I will not weary you with telling how I harassed myself and my husband, who was, however, scarce less interested, with doubts and conjectures. Suffice it that, next morning, P. came and took us in a carriage to a distant church. We had just entered the porch when a cart, such as fruit and vegetables are brought to market in, drove up, containing an elderly woman and a young girl. P. assisted them to alight, and advanced with the girl to the altar.

The girl was neatly dressed and quite handsome, yet, something in her expression displeased me the moment I looked upon her. Meanwhile the ceremony was going on, and, at its close, P. introduced us to the bride, and we all went to the door.

Good-by, Fanny, said the elderly woman. The new-made Mrs. P. replied without any token of affection or emotion. The woman got into the cart and drove away.

From that time I saw but little of P. or his wife. I took our mutual friends to see her, and they were civil to her for his sake. Curiosity was very much excited, but entirely baffled; no one, of course, dared speak to P. on the subject, and no other means could be found of solving the riddle.

He treated his wife with grave and kind politeness, but it was always obvious that they had nothing in common between them. Her manners and tastes were not at that time gross, but her character showed itself hard and material. She was fond of riding, and spent much time so. Her style in this, and in dress, seemed the opposite of P.'s; but he indulged all her wishes, while, for himself, he plunged into his own pursuits.

For a time he seemed, if not happy, not positively unhappy; but, after a few years, Mrs. P. fell into the habit of drinking, and then such scenes as you witnessed grew frequent. I have often heard of them, and always that P. sat, as you describe him, his head bowed down and perfectly silent all through, whatever might be done or whoever be present, and always his aspect has inspired such sympathy that no person has questioned him or resented her insults, but merely got out of the way, so soon as possible.

Hard and long penance, said my father, after some minutes musing, for an hour of passion, probably for his only error.

Is that your explanation? said the lady. O, improbable. P. might err, but not be led beyond himself.

I know his cool gray eye and calm complexion seemed to say so, but a different story is told by the lip that could tremble, and showed what flashes might pierce those deep blue heavens; and when these over intellectual beings do swerve aside, it is to fall down a precipice, for their narrow path lies over such. But he was not one to sin without making a brave atonement, and that it had become a holy one, was written on that downcast brow.

The fourth day on these waters, the weather was milder and brighter, so that we could now see them to some purpose. At night was clear moon, and, for the first time, from the upper deck, I saw one of the great steamboats come majestically up. It was glowing with lights, looking many-eyed and sagacious; in its heavy motion it seemed a dowager queen, and this motion, with its solemn pulse, and determined sweep, becomes these smooth waters, especially at night, as much as the dip of the sail-ship the long billows of the ocean.

But it was not so soon that I learned to appreciate the lake scenery; it was only after a daily and careless familiarity that I entered into its beauty, for nature always refuses to be seen by being stared at. Like Bonaparte, she discharges her face of all expression when she catches the eye of impertinent curiosity fixed on her. But he who has gone to sleep in childish ease on her lap, or leaned an aching brow upon her breast, seeking there comfort with full trust as from a mother, will see all a mother's beauty in the look she bends upon him. Later, I felt that I had really seen these regions, and shall speak of them again.

In the afternoon we went on shore at the Manitou islands, where the boat stops to wood. No one lives here except woodcutters for the steamboats. I had thought of such a position, from its mixture of profound solitude with service to the great world, as possessing an ideal beauty. I think so still, after seeing the woodcutters and their slovenly huts.

In times of slower growth, man did not enter a situation without a certain preparation or adaptedness to it. He drew from it, if not to the poetical extent, at least, in some proportion, its moral and its meaning. The woodcutter did not cut down so many trees a day, that the hamadryads had not time to make their plaints heard; the shepherd tended his sheep, and did no jobs or chores the while; the idyl had a chance to grow up, and modulate his oaten pipe. But now the poet must be at the whole expense of the poetry in describing one of these positions; the worker is a true Midas to the gold he makes. The poet must describe, as the painter sketches Irish peasant girls and Danish fishwives, adding the beauty, and leaving out the dirt.

I come to the west prepared for the distaste I must experience at its mushroom growth. I know that where "go ahead" is the only motto, the village cannot grow into the gentle proportions that successive lives, and the gradations of experience involuntarily give. In older countries the house of the son grew from that of the father, as naturally as new joints on a bough. And the cathedral crowned the whole as naturally as the leafy summit the tree. This cannot be here. The march of peaceful is scarce less wanton than that of warlike invasion. The old landmarks are broken down, and the land, for a season, bears none, except of the rudeness of conquest and the needs of the day, whose bivouac fires blacken the sweetest forest glades. I have come prepared to see all this, to dislike it, but not with stupid narrowness to distrust or defame. On the contrary, while I will not be so obliging as to confound ugliness with beauty, discord with harmony, and laud and be contented with all I meet, when it conflicts with my best desires and tastes, I trust by reverent faith to woo the mighty meaning of the scene, perhaps to foresee the law by which a new order, a new poetry is to be evoked from this chaos, and with a curiosity as ardent, but not so selfish as that of Macbeth, to call up the apparitions of future kings from the strange ingredients of the witch's caldron. Thus, I will not grieve that all the noble trees are gone already from this island to feed this caldron, but believe it will have Medea's virtue, and reproduce them in the form of new intellectual growths, since centuries cannot again adorn the land with such.

On this most beautiful beach of smooth white pebbles, interspersed with agates and cornelians, for those who know how to find them, we stepped, not like the Indian, with some humble offering, which, if no better than an arrow-head or a little parched corn, would, he judged, please the Manitou, who looks only at the spirit in which it is offered. Our visit was so far for a religious purpose that one of our party went to inquire the fate of some Unitarian tracts left among the woodcutters a year or two before. But the old Manitou, though, daunted like his children by the approach of the fire-ships which he probably considered demons of a new dynasty, he had suffered his woods to be felled to feed their pride, had been less patient of an encroachment, which did not to him seem so authorized by the law of the strongest, and had scattered those leaves as carelessly as the others of that year.

But S. and I, like other emigrants, went not to give, but to get, to rifle the wood of flowers for the service of the fire-ship. We returned with a rich booty, among which was the uva ursi, whose leaves the Indians smoke, with the kinnick-kinnick, and which had then just put forth its highly-finished little blossoms, as pretty as those of the blueberry.

Passing along still further, I thought it would be well if the crowds assembled to stare from the various landings were still confined to the kinnick-kinnick, for almost all had tobacco written on their faces, their cheeks rounded with plugs, their eyes dull with its fumes. We reached Chicago on the evening of the sixth day, having been out five days and a half, a rather longer passage than usual at a favorable season of the year.

Chicago, June 20.
There can be no two places in the world more completely thoroughfares than this place and Buffalo. They are the two correspondent valves that open and shut all the time, as the life-blood rushes from east to west, and back again from west to east.

Since it is their office thus to be the doors, and let in and out, it would be unfair to expect from them much character of their own. To make the best provisions for the transmission of produce is their office, and the people who live there are such as are suited for this; active, complaisant, inventive, business people. There are no provisions for the student or idler; to know what the place can give, you should be at work with the rest, the mere traveller will not find it profitable to loiter there as I did.

Since circumstances made it necessary for me so to do, I read all the books I could find about the new region, which now began to become real to me. All the books about the Indians, a paltry collection, truly, yet which furnished material for many thoughts. The most narrow-minded and awkward recital, still bears some lineaments of the great features of this nature, and the races of men that illustrated them.

Catlin's book is far the best. I was afterwards assured by those acquainted with the regions he describes, that he is not to be depended on for the accuracy of his facts, and, indeed, it is obvious, without the aid of such assertions, that he sometimes yields to the temptation of making out a story. They admitted, however, what from my feelings I was sure of, that he is true to the spirit of the scene, and that a far better view can be got from him than from any source at present existing, of the Indian tribes of the far west, and of the country where their inheritance lay.

Murray's travels I read, and was charmed by their accuracy and clear broad tone. He is the only Englishman that seems to have traversed these regions, as man, simply, not as John Bull. He deserves to belong to an aristocracy, for he showed his title to it more when left without a guide in the wilderness, than he can at the court of Victoria. He has, himself, no poetic force at description, but it is easy to make images from his hints. Yet we believe the Indian cannot be looked at truly except by a poetic eye. The Pawnees, no doubt, are such as he describes them, filthy in their habits, and treacherous in their character, but some would have seen, and seen truly, more beauty and dignity than he does with all his manliness and fairness of mind. However, his one fine old man is enough to redeem the rest, and is perhaps the relic of a better day, a Phocion among the Pawnees.

Schoolcraft's Algic Researches is a valuable book, though a worse use could hardly have been made of such fine material. Had the mythological or hunting stones of the Indians been written down exactly as they were received from the lips of the narrators, the collection could not have been surpassed in interest, both for the wild charm they carry with them, and the light they throw on a peculiar modification of life and mind. As it is, though the incidents have an air of originality and pertinence to the occasion, that gives us confidence that they have not been altered, the phraseology in which they were expressed has been entirely set aside, and the flimsy graces, common to the style of annuals and souvenirs, substituted for the Spartan brevity and sinewy grasp of Indian speech. We can just guess what might have been there, as we can detect the fine proportions of the Brave whom the bad taste of some white patron has arranged in frock-coat, hat, and pantaloons.

The few stories Mrs. Jameson wrote out, though to these also a sentimental air has been given, offend much less in that way than is common in this book. What would we give for a completely faithful version of some among them. Yet with all these drawbacks we cannot doubt from internal evidence that they truly ascribe to the Indian a delicacy of sentiment and of fancy that justifies Cooper in such inventions as his Uncas. It is a white man's view of a savage hero, who would be far finer in his natural proportions; still, through a masquerade figure, it implies the truth.

Irving's books I also read, some for the first, some for the second time, with increased interest, now that I was to meet such people as he received his materials from. Though the books are pleasing from their grace and luminous arrangement, yet, with the exception of the Tour to the Prairies, they have a stereotype, second-hand air. They lack the breath, the glow, the charming minute traits of living presence. His scenery is only fit to be glanced at from dioramic distance; his Indians are academic figures only. He would have made the best of pictures, if he could have used his own eyes for studies and sketches; as it is, his success is wonderful, but inadequate.

McKenney's Tour to the Lakes is the dullest of books, yet faithful and quiet, and gives some facts not to be met with elsewhere.

I also read a collection of Indian anecdotes and speeches, the worst compiled and arranged book possible, yet not without clues of some value. All these books I read in anticipation of a canoe-voyage on Lake Superior as far as the Pictured Rocks, and, though I was afterwards compelled to give up this project, they aided me in judging of what I afterwards saw and heard of the Indians.

In Chicago I first saw the beautiful prairie flowers. They were in their glory the first ten days we were there--

"The golden and the flame-like flowers."

The flame-like flower I was taught afterwards, by an Indian girl, to call "Wick-apee;" and she told me, too, that its splendors had a useful side, for it was used by the Indians as a remedy for an illness to which they were subject.

Beside these brilliant flowers, which gemmed and gilt the grass in a sunny afternoon's drive near the blue lake, between the low oakwood and the narrow beach, stimulated, whether sensuously by the optic nerve, unused to so much gold and crimson with such tender green, or symbolically through some meaning dimly seen in the flowers, I enjoyed a sort of fairyland exultation never felt before, and the first drive amid the flowers gave me anticipation of the beauty of the prairies.

At first, the prairie seemed to speak of the very desolation of dullness. After sweeping over the vast monotony of the lakes to come to this monotony of land, with all around a limitless horizon,--to walk, and walk, and run, but never climb, oh! it was too dreary for any but a Hollander to bear. How the eye greeted the approach of a sail, or the smoke of a steamboat; it seemed that any thing so animated must come from a better land, where mountains gave religion to the scene.

The only thing I liked at first to do, was to trace with slow and unexpecting step the narrow margin of the lake. Sometimes a heavy swell gave it expression; at others, only its varied coloring, which I found more admirable every day, and which gave it an air of mirage instead of the vastness of ocean. Then there was a grandeur in the feeling that I might continue that walk, if I had any seven-leagued mode of conveyance to save fatigue, for hundreds of miles without an obstacle and without a change.

But after I had rode out, and seen the flowers and seen the sun set with that calmness seen only in the prairies, and the cattle winding slowly home to their homes in the "island groves"--peacefullest of sights--I began to love because I began to know the scene, and shrank no longer from "the encircling vastness."

It is always thus with the new form of life; we must learn to look at it by its own standard. At first, no doubt my accustomed eye kept saying, if the mind did not, What! no distant mountains? what, no valleys? But after a while I would ascend the roof of the house where we lived, and pass many hours, needing no sight but the moon reigning in the heavens, or starlight falling upon the lake, till all the lights were out in the island grove of men beneath my feet, and felt nearer heaven that there was nothing but this lovely, still reception on the earth; no towering mountains, no deep tree-shadows, nothing but plain earth and water bathed in light.

Sunset, as seen from that place, presented most generally, low-lying, flaky clouds, of the softest serenity, "like," said S., "the Buddhist tracts."

One night a star shot madly from its sphere, and it had a fair chance to be seen, but that serenity could not be astonished.

Yes! it was a peculiar beauty of those sunsets and moonlights on the levels of Chicago which Chamouny or the Trosachs could not make me forget.

Notwithstanding all the attractions I thus found out by degrees on the flat shores of the lake, I was delighted when I found myself really on my way into the country for an excursion of two or three weeks. We set forth in a strong wagon, almost as large, and with the look of those used elsewhere for transporting caravans of wild beasteses, loaded with every thing we might want, in case nobody would give it to us--for buying and selling were no longer to be counted on--with a pair of strong horses, able and willing to force their way through mud holes and amid stumps, and a guide, equally admirable as marshal and companion, who knew by heart the country and its history, both natural and artificial, and whose clear hunter's eye needed neither road nor goal to guide it to all the spots where beauty best loves to dwell.

Add to this the finest weather, and such country as I had never seen, even in my dreams, although these dreams had been haunted by wishes for just such an one, and you may judge whether years of dullness might not, by these bright days, be redeemed, and a sweetness be shed over all thoughts of the West.

The first day brought us through woods rich in the moccasin flower and lupine, and plains whose soft expanse was continually touched with expression by the slow moving clouds which

> "Sweep over with their shadows, and beneath
> The surface rolls and fluctuates to the eye;
> Dark hollows seem to glide along and chase
>   The sunny ridges,"

to the banks of the Fox river, a sweet and graceful stream. We reached Geneva just in time to escape being drenched by a violent thunder shower, whose rise and disappearance threw expression into all the features of the scene.

Geneva reminds me of a New England village, as indeed there, and in the neighborhood, are many New Englanders of an excellent stamp, generous, intelligent, discreet, and seeking to win from life its true values. Such are much wanted, and seem like points of light among the swarms of settlers, whose aims are sordid, whose habits thoughtless and slovenly.

With great pleasure we heard, with his attentive and affectionate congregation, the Unitarian clergyman, Mr. Conant, and afterward visited him in his house, where almost everything bore traces of his own handy work or that of his father. He is just such a teacher as is wanted in this region, familiar enough with the habits of those he addresses to come home to their experience and their wants; earnest and enlightened enough to draw the important inferences from the life of every day.

A day or two we remained here, and passed some happy hours in the woods that fringe the stream, where the gentlemen found a rich booty of fish.

Next day, travelling along the river's banks, was an uninterrupted pleasure. We closed our drive in the afternoon at the house of an English gentleman, who has gratified, as few men do, the common wish to pass the evening of an active day amid the quiet influences of country life. He showed us a bookcase filled with books about this country; these he had collected for years, and become so familiar with the localities that, on coming here at last, he sought and found, at once, the very spot he wanted, and where he is as content as he hoped to be, thus realizing Wordsworth's description of the wise man, who "sees what he foresaw."

A wood surrounds the house, through which paths are cut in every direction. It is, for this new country, a large and handsome dwelling; but round it are its barns and farm yard, with cattle and poultry. These, however, in the framework of wood, have a very picturesque and pleasing effect. There is that mixture of culture and rudeness in the aspect of things as gives a feeling of freedom, not of confusion.

I wish it were possible to give some idea of this scene as viewed by the earliest freshness of dewy dawn. This habitation of man seemed like a nest in the grass, so thoroughly were the buildings and all the objects of human care harmonized with what was natural. The tall trees bent and whispered all around, as if to hail with sheltering love the men who had come to dwell among them.

The young ladies were musicians, and spoke French fluently, having been educated in a convent. Here in the prairie, they had learned to take care of the milk-room, and kill the rattlesnakes that assailed their poultry yard. Beneath the shade of heavy curtains you looked out from the high and large windows to see Norwegian peasants at work in their national dress. In the wood grew, not only the flowers I had before seen, and wealth of tall, wild roses, but the splendid blue spiderwort, that ornament of our gardens. Beautiful children strayed there, who were soon to leave these civilized regions for some really wild and western place, a post in the buffalo country. Their no less beautiful mother was of Welsh descent, and the eldest child bore the name of Gwynthleon. Perhaps there she will meet with some young descendants of Madoc, to be her friends; at any rate, her looks may retain that sweet, wild beauty, that is soon made to vanish from eyes which look too much on shops and streets, and the vulgarities of city "parties."

Next day we crossed the river. We ladies crossed on a little foot-bridge, from which we could look down the stream, and see the wagon pass over at the ford. A black thunder cloud was coming up. The sky and waters heavy with expectation. The motion of the wagon, with its white cover, and the laboring horses, gave just the due interest to the picture, because it seemed as if they would not have time to cross before the storm came on. However, they did get across, and we were a mile or two on our way before the violent shower obliged us to take refuge in a solitary house upon the prairie. In this country it is as pleasant to stop as to go on, to lose your way as to find it, for the variety in the population gives you a chance for fresh entertainment in every hut, and the luxuriant beauty makes every path attractive. In this house we found a family "quite above the common," but, I grieve to say, not above false pride, for the father, ashamed of being caught barefoot, told us a story of a man, one of the richest men, he said, in one of the eastern cities, who went barefoot, from choice and taste.

Near the door grew a Provence rose, then in blossom. Other families we saw had brought with them and planted the locust. It was pleasant to see their old home loves, brought into connection with their new splendors. Wherever there were traces of this tenderness of feeling, only too rare among Americans, other things bore signs also of prosperity and intelligence, as if the ordering mind of man had some idea of home beyond a mere shelter, beneath which to eat and sleep.

No heaven need wear a lovelier aspect than earth did this afternoon, after the clearing up of the shower. We traversed the blooming plain, unmarked by any road, only the friendly track of wheels which tracked, not broke the grass. Our stations were not from town to town, but from grove to grove. These groves first floated like blue islands in the distance. As we drew nearer, they seemed fair parks, and the little log houses on the edge, with their curling smokes, harmonized beautifully with them.

One of these groves, Ross's grove, we reached just at sunset. It was of the noblest trees I saw during this journey, for the trees generally were not large or lofty, but only of fair proportions. Here they were large enough to form with their clear stems pillars for grand cathedral aisles. There was space enough for crimson light to stream through upon the floor of water which the shower had left. As we slowly plashed through, I thought I was never in a better place for vespers.

That night we rested, or rather tarried at a grove some miles beyond, and there partook of the miseries so often jocosely portrayed, of bedchambers for twelve, a milk dish for universal handbasin, and expectations that you would use and lend your "hankercher" for a towel. But this was the only night, thanks to the hospitality of private families, that we passed thus, and it was well that we had this bit of experience, else might we have pronounced all Trollopian records of the kind to be inventions of pure malice.

With us was a 'young lady who showed herself to have been bathed in the Britannic fluid, wittily described by a late French writer, by the impossibility she experienced of accommodating herself to the indecorums of the scene. We ladies were to sleep in the bar-room, from which its drinking visitors could be ejected only at a late hour. The outer door had no fastening to prevent their return. However, our host kindly requested we would call him, if they did, as he had "conquered them for us," and would do so again. We had also rather hard couches; (mine was the supper table,) but we yankees, born to rove, were altogether too much fatigued to stand upon trifles, and slept as sweetly as we would in the "bigly bower" of any baroness. But I think England sat up all night, wrapped in her blanket shawl, and with a neat lace cap upon her head; so that she would have looked perfectly the lady, if any one had come in; shuddering and listening. I know that she was very ill next day, in requital. She watched, as her parent country watches the seas, that nobody may do wrong in any case, and deserved to have met some interruption, she was so well prepared. However, there was none, other than from the nearness of some twenty sets of powerful lungs, which would not leave the night to a deadly stillness. In this house we had, if not good beds, yet good tea, good bread, and wild strawberries, and were entertained with most free communications of opinion and history from our hosts. Neither shall any of us have a right to say again that we cannot find any who may be willing to hear all we may have to say. "A's fish that comes to the net," should be painted on the sign at Papaw grove.

CHAPTER III.

In the afternoon of this day we reached the Rock river, in whose neighborhood we proposed to make some stay, and crossed at Dixon's ferry.

This beautiful stream flows full and wide over a bed of rocks, traversing a distance of near two hundred miles, to reach the Mississippi. Great part of the country along its banks is the finest region of Illinois, and the scene of some of the latest romance of Indian warfare. To these beautiful regions Black Hawk returned with his band "to pass the summer," when he drew upon himself the warfare in which he was finally vanquished. No wonder he could not resist the longing, unwise though its indulgence might be, to return in summer to this home of beauty.

Of Illinois, in general, it has often been remarked that it bears the character of country which has been inhabited by a nation skilled like the English in all the ornamental arts of life, especially in landscape gardening. That the villas and castles seem to have been burnt, the enclosures taken down, but the velvet lawns, the flower gardens, the stately parks, scattered at graceful intervals by the decorous hand of art, the frequent deer, and the peaceful herd of cattle that make picture of the plain, all suggest more of the masterly mind of man, than the prodigal, but careless, motherly love of nature. Especially is this true of the Rock river country. The river flows sometimes through these parks and lawns, then betwixt high bluffs, whose grassy ridges are covered with fine trees, or broken with crumbling stone, that easily assumes, the forms of buttress, arch and clustered columns. Along the face of such crumbling rocks, swallows' nests are clustered, thick as cities, and eagles and deer do not disdain their summits. One morning, out in the boat along the base of these rocks, it was amusing, and affecting too, to see these swallows put their heads out to look at us. There was something very hospitable about it, as if man had never shown himself a tyrant near them. What a morning that was! Every sight is worth twice as much by the early morning light. We borrow something of the spirit of the hour to look upon them.

The first place, where we stopped was one of singular beauty, a beauty of soft, luxuriant wildness. It was on the bend of the river, a place chosen by an Irish gentleman, whose absenteeship seems of the wisest kind, since for a sum which would have been but a drop of water to the thirsty fever of his native land, he commands a residence which has all that is desirable, in its independence, its beautiful retirement, and means of benefit to others.

His park, his deer-chase, he found already prepared; he had only to make an avenue through it. This brought us by a drive, which in the heat of noon seemed long, though afterwards, in the cool of morning and evening, delightful, to the house. This is, for that part of the world, a large and commodious dwelling. Near it stands the log-cabin where its master lived while it was building, a very ornamental accessory.

In front of the house was a lawn, adorned by the most graceful trees. A few of these had been taken out to give a full view of the river, gliding through banks such as I have described. On this bend the bank is high and bold, so from the house or the lawn the view was very rich and commanding. But if you descended a ravine at the side to the water's edge, you found there a long walk on the narrow shore, with a wall above of the richest hanging wood, in which they said the deer lay hid. I never saw one, but often fancied that I heard them rustling, at daybreak, by these bright clear waters, stretching out in such smiling promise, where no sound broke the deep and blissful seclusion, unless now and then this rustling, or the plash of some fish a little gayer than the others; it seemed not necessary to have any better heaven, or fuller expression of love and freedom than in the mood of nature here.

Then, leaving the bank, you would walk far and far through long grassy paths, full of the most brilliant, also the most delicate flowers. The brilliant are more common on the prairie, but both kinds loved this place.

Amid the grass of the lawn, with a profusion of wild strawberries, we greeted also a familiar love, the Scottish harebell, the gentlest, and most touching form of the flower-world.

The master of the house was absent, but with a kindness beyond thanks had offered us a resting place there. Here we were taken care of by a deputy, who would, for his youth, have been assigned the place of a page in former times, but in the young west, it seems he was old enough for a steward. Whatever be called his function, he did the honors of the place so much in harmony with it, as to leave the guests free to imagine themselves in Elysium. And the three days passed here were days of unalloyed, spotless happiness.

There was a peculiar charm in coming here, where the choice of location, and the unobtrusive good taste of all the arrangements, showed such intelligent appreciation of the spirit of the scene, after seeing so many dwellings of the new settlers, which showed plainly that they had no thought beyond satisfying the grossest material wants. Sometimes they looked attractive, the little brown houses, the natural architecture of the country, in the edge of the timber. But almost always when you came near, the slovenliness of the dwelling and the rude way in which objects around it were treated, when so little care would have presented a charming whole, were very repulsive. Seeing the traces of the Indians, who chose the most beautiful sites for their dwellings, and whose habits do not break in on that aspect of nature under which they were born, we feel as if they were the rightful lords of a beauty they forbore to deform. But most of these settlers do not see it at all; it breathes, it speaks in vain to those who are rushing into its sphere. Their progress is Gothic, not Roman, and their mode of cultivation will, in the course of twenty, perhaps ten, years, obliterate the natural expression of the country.

This is inevitable, fatal; we must not complain, but look forward to a good result. Still, in travelling through this country, I could not but be struck with the force of a symbol. Wherever the hog comes, the rattlesnake disappears; the omnivorous traveller, safe in its stupidity, willingly and easily makes a meal of the most dangerous of reptiles, and one whom the Indian looks on with a mystic awe. Even so the white settler pursues the Indian, and is victor in the chase. But I shall say more upon the subject by-and-by.

While we were here we had one grand thunder storm, which added new glory to the scene.

One beautiful feature was the return of the pigeons every afternoon to their home. Every afternoon they came sweeping across the lawn, positively in clouds, and with a swiftness and softness of winged motion, more beautiful than anything of the kind I ever knew. Had I been a musician, such as Mendelsohn, I felt that I could have improvised a music quite peculiar, from the sound they made, which should have indicated all the beauty over which their wings bore them. I will here insert a few lines left at this house, on parting, which feebly indicate some of the features.

>Familiar to the childish mind were tales
> Of rock-girt isles amid a desert sea,
>Where unexpected stretch the flowery vales
> To soothe the shipwrecked sailor's misery.
>Fainting, he lay upon a sandy shore,
>And fancied that all hope of life was o'er;
>But let him patient climb the frowning wall,
>Within, the orange glows beneath the palm tree tall,
>And all that Eden boasted waits his call.
>
>Almost these tales seem realized to-day,
>When the long dullness of the sultry way,
>Where "independent" settlers' careless cheer
>Made us indeed feel we were "strangers" here,
>Is cheered by sudden sight of this fair spot,
>On which "improvement" yet has made no blot,
>But Nature all-astonished stands, to find
>Her plan protected by the human mind.
>
>Blest be the kindly genius of the scene;
> The river, bending in unbroken grace,
>The stately thickets, with their pathways green,
> Fair lonely trees, each in its fittest place.
>Those thickets haunted by the deer and fawn;
>Those cloudlike flights of birds across the lawn;
>The gentlest breezes here delight to blow,
>And sun and shower and star are emulous to deck the show.

Wondering, as Crusoe, we survey the land;
Happier than Crusoe we, a friendly band;
Blest be the hand that reared this friendly home,
The heart and mind of him to whom we owe
Hours of pure peace such as few mortals know;
May he find such, should he be led to roam;
Be tended by such ministering sprites--
Enjoy such gaily childish days, such hopeful nights!
And yet, amid the goods to mortals given,
To give those goods again is most like heaven.

Hazelwood, Rock River, June 30th, 1843.

The only really rustic feature was of the many coops of poultry near the house, which I understood it to be one of the chief pleasures of the master to feed.

Leaving this place, we proceeded a day's journey along the beautiful stream, to a little town named Oregon. We called at a cabin, from whose door looked out one of those faces which, once seen, are never forgotten; young, yet touched with many traces of feeling, not only possible, but endured; spirited, too, like the gleam of a finely tempered blade. It was a face that suggested a history, and many histories, but whose scene would have been in courts and camps. At this moment their circles are dull for want of that life which is waning unexcited in this solitary recess.

The master of the house proposed to show us a "short cut," by which we might, to especial advantage, pursue our journey. This proved to be almost perpendicular down a hill, studded with young trees and stumps. From these he proposed, with a hospitality of service worthy an Oriental, to free our wheels whenever they should get entangled, also, to be himself the drag, to prevent our too rapid descent. Such generosity deserved trust; however, we women could not be persuaded to render it. We got out and admired, from afar, the process. Left by our guide--and prop! we found ourselves in a wide field, where, by playful quips and turns, an endless "creek," seemed to divert itself with our attempts to cross it. Failing in this, the next best was to whirl down a steep bank, which feat our charioteer performed with an air not unlike that of Rhesus, had he but been as suitably furnished with chariot and steeds!

At last, after wasting some two or three hours on the "short cut," we got out by following an Indian trail,--Black Hawk's! How fair the scene through which it led! How could they let themselves be conquered, with such a country to fight for!

Afterwards, in the wide prairie, we saw a lively picture of nonchalance, (to speak in the fashion of dear Ireland.) There, in the wide sunny field, with neither tree nor umbrella above his head, sat a pedler, with his pack, waiting apparently for customers. He was not disappointed. We bought, what hold in regard to the human world, as unmarked, as mysterious, and as important an existence, as the infusoria to the natural, to wit, pins. This incident would have delighted those modern sages, who, in imitation of the sitting philosophers of ancient Ind, prefer silence to speech, waiting to going, and scornfully smile in answer to the motions of earnest life,

"Of itself will nothing come,
That ye must still be seeking?"

However, it seemed to me to-day, as formerly on these sublime occasions, obvious that nothing would come, unless something would go; now, if we had been as sublimely still as the pedler, his pins would have tarried in the pack, and his pockets sustained an aching void of pence!

Passing through one of the fine, park-like woods, almost clear from underbrush and carpeted with thick grasses and flowers, we met, (for it was Sunday,) a little congregation just returning from their service, which had been performed in a rude house in its midst. It had a sweet and peaceful air, as if such words and thoughts were very dear to them. The parents had with them all their little children; but we saw no old people; that charm was wanting, which exists in such scenes in older settlements, of seeing the silver bent in reverence beside the flaxen head.

At Oregon, the beauty of the scene was of even a more sumptuous character than at our former "stopping place." Here swelled the river in its boldest course, interspersed by halcyon isles on which nature had lavished all her prodigality in tree, vine, and flower, banked by noble bluffs, three hundred feet high, their sharp ridges as exquisitely definite as the edge of a shell; their summits adorned with those same beautiful trees, and with buttresses of rich rock, crested with old hemlocks, which wore a touching and antique grace amid the softer and more luxuriant vegetation. Lofty natural mounds rose amidst the rest, with the same lovely and sweeping outline, showing everywhere the plastic power of water,--water, mother of beauty, which, by its sweet and eager flow, had left such lineaments as human genius never dreamt of.

Not far from the river was a high crag, called the Pine Rock, which looks out, as our guide observed, like a helmet above the brow of the country. It seems as if the water left here and there a vestige of forms and materials that preceded its course, just to set off its new and richer designs.

The aspect of this country was to me enchanting, beyond any I have ever seen, from its fullness of expression, its bold and impassioned sweetness. Here the flood of emotion has passed over and marked everywhere its course by a smile. The fragments of rock touch it with a wildness and liberality which give just the needed relief. I should never be tired here, though I have elsewhere seen country of more secret and alluring charms, better calculated to stimulate and suggest. Here the eye and heart are filled.

How happy the Indians must have been here! It is not long since they were driven away, and the ground, above and below, is full of their traces.

"The earth is full of men."

You have only to turn up the sod to find arrowheads and Indian pottery. On an island, belonging to our host, and nearly opposite his house, they loved to stay, and, no doubt, enjoyed its lavish beauty as much as the myriad wild pigeons that now haunt its flower-filled shades. Here are still the marks of their tomahawks, the troughs in which they prepared their corn, their caches.

A little way down the river is the site of an ancient Indian village, with its regularly arranged mounds. As usual, they had chosen with the finest taste. It was one of those soft shadowy afternoons when we went there, when nature seems ready to weep, not from grief, but from an overfull heart. Two prattling, lovely little girls, and an African boy, with glittering eye and ready grin, made our party gay; but all were still as we entered their little inlet and trod those flowery paths. They may blacken Indian life as they will, talk of its dirt, its brutality, I will ever believe that the men who chose that dwelling-place were able to feel emotions of noble happiness as they returned to it, and so were the women that received them. Neither were the children sad or dull, who lived so familiarly with the deer and the birds, and swam that clear wave in the shadow of the Seven Sisters. The whole scene suggested to me a Greek splendor, a Greek sweetness, and I can believe that an Indian brave, accustomed to ramble in such paths, and be bathed by such sunbeams, might be mistaken for Apollo, as Apollo was for him by West. Two of the boldest bluffs are called the Deer's Walk, (not because deer do *not* walk there,) and the Eagle's Nest. The latter I visited one glorious morning; it was that, of the fourth of July, and certainly I think I had never felt so happy that I was born in America. Wo to all country folks that never saw this spot, never swept an enraptured gaze over the prospect that stretched beneath. I do believe Rome and Florence are suburbs compared to this capital of nature's art.

The bluff was decked with great bunches of a scarlet variety of the milkweed, like cut coral, and all starred with a mysterious-looking dark flower, whose cup rose lonely on a tall stem. This had, for two or three days, disputed the ground with the lupine and phlox. My companions disliked, I liked it.

Here I thought of, or rather saw, what the Greek expresses under the form of Jove's darling, Ganymede, and the following stanzas took form.

GANYMEDE TO HIS EAGLE,

SUGGESTED BY A WORK OF THORWALDSEN'S.

Composed on the height called the Eagle's Nest, Oregon, Rock River,

July 4th, 1843.

Upon the rocky mountain stood the boy,
  A goblet of pure water in his hand,
His face and form spoke him one made for joy,

A willing servant to sweet love's command,
But a strange pain was written on his brow,
And thrilled throughout his silver accents now--

"My bird," he cries, "my destined brother friend,
  O whither fleets to-day thy wayward flight?
Hast thou forgotten that I here attend,
  From the full noon until this sad twilight?
A hundred times, at least, from the clear spring,
Since the full noon o'er hill and valley glowed,
I've filled the vase which our Olympian king
  Upon my care for thy sole use bestowed;
That at the moment when thou should'st descend,
A pure refreshment might thy thirst attend.

Hast thou forgotten earth, forgotten me,
  Thy fellow bondsman in a royal cause,
Who, from the sadness of infinity,
  Only with thee can know that peaceful pause
In which we catch the flowing strain of love,
Which binds our dim fates to the throne of Jove?

Before I saw thee, I was like the May,
  Longing for summer that must mar its bloom,
Or like the morning star that calls the day,
  Whose glories to its promise are the tomb;
And as the eager fountain rises higher
  To throw itself more strongly back to earth,
Still, as more sweet and full rose my desire,
  More fondly it reverted to its birth,
For, what the rosebud seeks tells not the rose,
The meaning foretold by the boy the man cannot disclose.

I was all Spring, for in my being dwelt
  Eternal youth, where flowers are the fruit,
Full feeling was the thought of what was felt,
  Its music was the meaning of the lute;
But heaven and earth such life will still deny,
For earth, divorced from heaven, still asks the question ***Why?***

Upon the highest mountains my young feet
  Ached, that no pinions from their lightness grew,
My starlike eyes the stars would fondly greet,
  Yet win no greeting from the circling blue;
Fair, self-subsistent each in its own sphere,
  They had no care that there was none for me;
Alike to them that I was far or near,
  Alike to them, time and eternity.

But, from the violet of lower air,
  Sometimes an answer to my wishing came,
Those lightning births my nature seemed to share,
  They told the secrets of its fiery frame,
The sudden messengers of hate and love,
The thunderbolts that arm the hand of Jove,
And strike sometimes the sacred spire, and strike the sacred grove.

Come in a moment, in a moment gone,
They answered me, then left me still more lone,
They told me that the thought which ruled the world,
As yet no sail upon its course had furled,
That the creation was but just begun,
New leaves still leaving from the primal one,
But spoke not of the goal to which ***my*** rapid wheels would run.

Still, still my eyes, though tearfully, I strained
To the far future which my heart contained,
And no dull doubt my proper hope profaned.

At last, O bliss, thy living form I spied,
  Then a mere speck upon a distant sky,
Yet my keen glance discerned its noble pride,
  And the full answer of that sun-filled eye;
I knew it was the wing that must upbear
My earthlier form into the realms of air.

Thou knowest how we gained that beauteous height,
Where dwells the monarch of the sons of light,
Thou knowest he declared us two to be
The chosen servants of his ministry,
Thou as his messenger, a sacred sign
Of conquest, or with omen more benign,
To give its due weight to the righteous cause,
To express the verdict of Olympian laws.

And I to wait upon the lonely spring,
  Which slakes the thirst of bards to whom 'tis given
The destined dues of hopes divine to sing,
  And weave the needed chain to bind to heaven.
Only from such could be obtained a draught
For him who in his early home from Jove's own cup has quaffed.

To wait, to wait, but not to wait too long,
Till heavy grows the burthen of a song;
O bird! too long hast thou been gone to-day,
My feet are weary of their frequent way,
The spell that opes the spring my tongue no more can say.

If soon thou com'st not, night will fall around,
My head with a sad slumber will be bound,
And the pure draught be spilt upon the ground.

Remember that I am not yet divine,
Long years of service to the fatal Nine
Are yet to make a Delphian vigor mine.

O, make them not too hard, thou bird of Jove,
Answer the stripling's hope, confirm his love,
Receive the service in which he delights,
And bear him often to the serene heights,
Where hands that were so prompt in serving thee,
Shall be allowed the highest ministry,
And Rapture live with bright Fidelity.

The afternoon was spent in a very different manner. The family, whose guests we were, possessed a gay and graceful hospitality that gave zest to each moment. They possessed that rare politeness which, while fertile in pleasant expedients to vary the enjoyment of a friend, leaves him perfectly free the moment he wishes to be so. With such hosts, pleasure may be combined with repose. They lived on the bank opposite the town, and, as their house was full, we slept in the town, and passed three days with them, passing to and fro morning and evening in their boats. (To one of these, called the Fairy, in which a sweet little daughter of the house moved about lighter than any Scotch Ellen ever sung, I should indite a poem, if I had not been guilty of rhyme on the very last page.) At morning this was very pleasant; at evening, I confess I was generally too tired with the excitements of the day to think it so.

Their house--a double log cabin--was, to my eye, the model of a Western villa. Nature had laid out before it grounds which could not be improved. Within, female taste had veiled every rudeness--availed itself of every sylvan grace.

In this charming abode what laughter, what sweet thoughts, what pleasing fancies, did we not enjoy! May such never desert those who reared it and made us so kindly welcome to all its pleasures!

Fragments of city life were dexterously crumbled into the dish prepared for general entertainment. Ice creams followed the dinner drawn by the gentlemen from the river, and music and fireworks wound up the evening of days spent on the Eagle's Nest. Now they had prepared a little fleet to pass over to the Fourth of July celebration, which some queer drumming and fifing, from the opposite bank, had announced to be "on hand."

We found the free and independent citizens there collected beneath the trees, among whom many a round Irish visage dimpled at the usual puffs of Ameriky.

The orator was a New Englander, and the speech smacked loudly of Boston, but was received with much applause, and followed by a plentiful dinner, provided by and for the Sovereign People, to which Hail Columbia served as grace.

Returning, the gay flotilla hailed the little flag which the children had raised from a log-cabin, prettier than any president ever saw, and drank the health of their country and all mankind, with a clear conscience.

Dance and song wound up the day. I know not when the mere local habitation has seemed to me to afford so fair a chance of happiness as this. To a person of unspoiled tastes, the beauty alone would afford stimulus enough. But with it would be naturally associated all kinds of wild sports, experiments, and the studies of natural history. In these regards, the poet, the sportsman, the naturalist, would alike rejoice in this wide range of untouched loveliness.

Then, with a very little money, a ducal estate may be purchased, and by a very little more, and moderate labor, a family be maintained upon it with raiment, food and shelter. The luxurious and minute comforts of a city life are not yet to be had without effort disproportionate to their value. But, where there is so great, a counterpoise, cannot these be given up once for all? If the houses are imperfectly built, they can afford immense fires and plenty of covering; if they are small, who cares?--with such fields to roam in. In winter, it may be borne; in summer, is of no consequence. With plenty of fish, and game, and wheat, can they not dispense with a baker to bring "muffins hot" every morning to the door for their breakfast?

Here a man need not take a small slice from the landscape, and fence it in from the obtrusions of an uncongenial neighbor, and there cut down his fancies to miniature improvements which a chicken could run over in ten minutes. He may have water and wood and land enough, to dread no incursions on his prospect from some chance Vandal that may enter his neighborhood. He need not painfully economise and manage how he may use it all; he can afford to leave some of it wild, and to carry out his own plans without obliterating those of nature.

Here, whole families might live together, if they would. The sons might return from their pilgrimages to settle near the parent hearth; the daughters might find room near their mother. Those painful separations, which already desecrate and desolate the Atlantic coast, are not enforced here by the stern need of seeking bread; and where they are voluntary, it is no matter. To me, too, used to the feelings which haunt a society of struggling men, it was delightful to look upon a scene where nature still wore her motherly smile and seemed to promise room not only for those favored or cursed with the qualities best adapting for the strifes of competition, but for the delicate, the thoughtful, even the indolent or eccentric. She did not say, Fight or starve; nor even, Work or cease to exist; but, merely showing that the apple was a finer fruit than the wild crab, gave both room to grow in the garden.

A pleasant society is formed of the families who live along the banks of this stream upon farms. They are from various parts of the world, and have much to communicate to one another. Many have cultivated minds and refined manners, all a varied experience, while they have in common the interests of a new country and a new life. They must traverse some space to get at one another, but the journey is through scenes that make it a separate pleasure. They must bear inconveniences to stay in one another's houses; but these, to the well-disposed, are only a source of amusement and adventure.

The great drawback upon the lives of these settlers, at present, is the unfitness of the women for their new lot. It has generally been the choice of the men, and the women follow, as women will, doing their best for affection's sake, but too often in heart-sickness and weariness. Beside it frequently not being a choice or conviction of their own minds that it is best to be here, their part is the hardest, and they are least fitted for it. The men can find assistance in field labor, and recreation with the gun and fishing-rod. Their bodily strength is greater, and enables them to bear and enjoy both these forms of life.

The women can rarely find any aid in domestic labor. All its various and careful tasks must often be performed, sick or well, by the mother and daughters, to whom a city education has imparted neither the strength nor skill now demanded.

The wives of the poorer settlers, having more hard work to do than before, very frequently become slatterns; but the ladies, accustomed to a refined neatness, feel that they cannot degrade themselves by its absence, and struggle under every disadvantage to keep up the necessary routine of small arrangements.

With all these disadvantages for work, their resources for pleasure are fewer. When they can leave the housework, they have not learnt to ride, to drive, to row, alone. Their culture has too generally been that given to women to make them "the ornaments of society." They can dance, but not draw; talk French, but know nothing of the language of flowers; neither in childhood were allowed to cultivate them, lest they should tan their complexions. Accustomed to the pavement of Broadway, they dare not tread the wild-wood paths for fear of rattlesnakes!

Seeing much of this joylessness, and inaptitude, both of body and mind, for a lot which would be full of blessings for those prepared for it, we could not but look with deep interest on the little girls, and hope they would grow up with the strength of body, dexterity, simple tastes, and resources that would fit them to enjoy and refine the western farmer's life.

But they have a great deal to war with in the habits of thought acquired by their mothers from their own early life. Everywhere the fatal spirit of imitation, of reference to European standards, penetrates, and threatens to blight whatever of original growth might adorn the soil.

If the little girls grow up strong, resolute, able to exert their faculties, their mothers mourn over their want of fashionable delicacy. Are they gay, enterprising, ready to fly about in the various ways that teach them so much, these ladies lament that "they cannot go to school, where they might learn to be quiet." They lament the want of "education" for their daughters, as if the thousand needs which call out their young energies, and the language of nature around, yielded no education.

Their grand ambition for their children, is to send them to school in some eastern city, the measure most likely to make them useless and unhappy at home. I earnestly hope that, ere long, the existence of good schools near themselves, planned by persons of sufficient thought to meet the wants of the place and time, instead of copying New York or Boston, will correct this mania. Instruction the children want to enable them to profit by the great natural advantages of their position; but methods copied from the education of some English Lady Augusta, are as ill suited to the daughter of an Illinois farmer, as satin shoes to climb the Indian mounds. An elegance she would diffuse around her, if her mind were opened to appreciate elegance; it might be of a kind new, original, enchanting, as different from that of the city belle as that of the prairie torch-flower from the shopworn article that touches the cheek of that lady within her bonnet.

To a girl really skilled to make home beautiful and comfortable, with bodily strength to enjoy plenty of exercise, the woods, the streams, a few studies, music, and the sincere and familiar intercourse, far more easily to be met here than elsewhere, would afford happiness enough. Her eyes would not grow dim, nor her cheeks sunken, in the absence of parties, morning visits, and milliner's shops.

As to music, I wish I could see in such places the guitar rather than the piano, and good vocal more than instrumental music.

The piano many carry with them, because it is the fashionable instrument in the eastern cities. Even there, it is so merely from the habit of imitating Europe, for not one in a thousand is willing to give the labor requisite to ensure any valuable use of the instrument.

But, out here, where the ladies have so much less leisure, it is still less desirable. Add to this, they never know how to tune their own instruments, and as persons seldom visit them who can do so, these pianos are constantly out of tune, and would spoil the ear of one who began by having any.

The guitar, or some portable instrument which requires less practice, and could be kept in tune by themselves, would be far more desirable for most of these ladies. It would give all they want as a household companion to fill up the gaps of life with a pleasant stimulus or solace, and be sufficient accompaniment to the voice in social meetings.

Singing in parts is the most delightful family amusement, and those who are constantly together can learn to sing in perfect accord. All the practice it needs, after some good elementary instruction, is such as meetings by summer twilight, and evening firelight naturally suggest. And, as music is an universal language, we cannot but think a fine Italian duet would be as much at home in the log cabin as one of Mrs. Gore's novels.

The sixth July we left this beautiful place. It was one of those rich days of bright sunlight, varied by the purple shadows of large sweeping clouds. Many a backward look we cast, and left the heart behind.

Our journey to-day was no less delightful than before, still all new, boundless, limitless. Kinmont says, that limits are sacred; that the Greeks were in the right to worship a god of limits. I say, that what is limitless is alone divine, that there was neither wall nor road in Eden, that those who walked there lost and found their way just as we did, and that all the gain from the Fall was that we had a wagon to ride in. I do not think, either, that even the horses doubted whether this last was any advantage.

Everywhere the rattlesnake-weed grows in profusion. The antidote survives the bane. Soon the coarser plantain, the "white man's footstep," shall take its place.

We saw also the compass plant, and the western tea plant. Of some of the brightest flowers an Indian girl afterwards told me the medicinal virtues. I doubt not those students of the soil knew a use to every fair emblem, on which we could only look to admire its hues and shape.

After noon we were ferried by a girl, (unfortunately not of the most picturesque appearance) across the Kishwaukie, the most graceful stream, and on whose bosom rested many full-blown water-lilies, twice as large as any of ours. I was told that, ***en revanche***, they were scentless, but I still regret that I could not get at one of them to try.

Query, did the lilied fragrance which, in the miraculous times, accompanied visions of saints and angels, proceed from water or garden lilies?

Kishwaukie is, according to tradition, the scene of a famous battle, and its many grassy mounds contain the bones of the valiant. On these waved thickly the mysterious purple flower, of which I have spoken before. I think it springs from the blood of the Indians, as the hyacinth did from that of Apollo's darling.

The ladies of our host's family at Oregon, when they first went there, after all the pains and plagues of building and settling, found their first pastime in opening one of these mounds, in which they found, I think, three of the departed, seated in the Indian fashion.

One of these same ladies, as she was making bread one winter morning, saw from the window a deer directly before the house. She ran out, with her hands covered with dough, calling the others, and they caught him bodily before he had time to escape.

Here (at Kishwaukie) we received a visit from a ragged and barefoot, but bright-eyed gentleman, who seemed to be the intellectual loafer, the walking Will's coffeehouse of the place. He told us many charming snake stories; among others, of himself having seen seventeen young ones reenter the mother snake, on the intrusion of a visiter.

This night we reached Belvidere, a flourishing town in Boon county, where was the tomb, now despoiled, of Big Thunder. In this later day we felt happy to find a really good hotel.

From this place, by two days of very leisurely and devious journeying, we reached Chicago, and thus ended a journey, which one at least of the party might have wished unending.

I have not been particularly anxious to give the geography of the scene, inasmuch as it seemed to me no route, nor series of stations, but a garden interspersed with cottages, groves and flowery lawns, through which a stately river ran. I had no guide-book, kept no diary, do not know how many miles we travelled each day, nor how many in all. What I got from the journey was the poetic impression of the country at large; it is all I have aimed to communicate.

The narrative might have been made much more interesting, as life was at the time, by many piquant anecdotes and tales drawn from private life. But here courtesy restrains the pen, for I know those who received the stranger with such frank kindness would feel ill requited by its becoming the means of fixing many spy-glasses, even though the scrutiny might be one of admiring interest, upon their private homes.

For many of these, too, I was indebted to a friend, whose property they more lawfully are. This friend was one of those rare beings who are equally at home in nature and with man. He knew a tale of all that ran and swam, and flew, or only grew, possessing that extensive familiarity with things which shows equal sweetness of sympathy and playful penetration. Most refreshing to me was his unstudied lore, the unwritten poetry which common life presents to a strong and gentle mind. It was a great contrast to the subtleties of analysis, the philosophic strainings of which I had seen too much. But I will not attempt to transplant it. May it profit others as it did me in the region where it was born, where it belongs. The evening of our return to Chicago the sunset was of a splendor and calmness beyond any we saw at the West. The twilight that succeeded was equally beautiful; soft, pathetic, but just so calm. When afterwards I learned this was the evening of Allston's death, it seemed to me as if this glorious pageant was not without connection with that event; at least, it inspired similar emotions,--a heavenly gate closing a path adorned with shows well worthy Paradise.

* * * * *

Farewell, ye soft and sumptuous solitudes! Ye fairy distances, ye lordly woods, Haunted by paths like those that Poussin knew, When after his all gazers eyes he drew; I go,--and if I never more may steep An eager heart in your enchantments deep, Yet ever to itself that heart may say, Be not exacting; thou hast lived one day; Hast looked on that which matches with thy mood, Impassioned sweetness of full being's flood, Where nothing checked the bold yet gentle wave, Where nought repelled the lavish love that gave. A tender blessing lingers o'er the scene, Like some young mother's thought, fond, yet serene, And through its life new-born our lives have been. Once more farewell,--a sad, a sweet farewell; And, if I never must behold you more, In other worlds I will not cease to tell The rosary I here have numbered o'er; And bright-haired Hope will lend a gladdened ear, And Love will free him from the grasp of Fear, And Gorgon critics, while the tale they hear, Shall dew their stony glances with a tear, If I but catch one echo from your spell;-- And so farewell,--a grateful, sad farewell!

CHAPTER IV.
CHICAGO AGAIN.

Chicago had become interesting to me now, that I knew it as the portal to so fair a scene. I had become interested in the land, in the people, and looked sorrowfully on the lake on which I must soon embark, to leave behind what I had just begun to enjoy.

Now was the time to see the lake. The July moon was near its full, and night after night it rose in a cloudless sky above this majestic sea. The heat was excessive, so that there was no enjoyment of life, except in the night, but then the air was of that delicious temperature, worthy of orange groves. However, they were not wanted;--nothing was, as that full light fell on the faintly rippling waters which then seemed boundless.

A poem received shortly after, from a friend in Massachusetts, seemed to say that the July moon shone there not less splendid, and may claim insertion here.

TRIFORMIS.

So pure her forehead's dazzling white,
  So swift and clear her radiant eyes,
Within the treasure of whose light
  Lay undeveloped destinies,--
Of thoughts repressed such hidden store
  Was hinted by each flitting smile,
I could but wonder and adore,
  Far off, in awe, I gazed the while.

I gazed at her, as at the moon,
  Hanging in lustrous twilight skies,
Whose virgin crescent, sinking soon,
  Peeps through the leaves before it flies.
Untouched Diana, flitting dim,
  While sings the wood its evening hymn.

II.

Again we met. O joyful meeting!
  Her radiance now was all for me,
Like kindly airs her kindly greeting,
  So full, so musical, so free.
Within romantic forest aisles,
  Within romantic paths we walked,
I bathed me in her sister smiles,
  I breathed her beauty as we talked.

So full-orbed Cynthia walks the skies,
  Filling the earth with melodies,
Even so she condescends to kiss
  Drowsy Endymions, coarse and dull,
Or fills our waking souls with bliss,
  Making long nights too beautiful.

III.

O fair, but fickle lady-moon,
  Why must thy full form ever wane?
O love! O friendship! why so soon
  Must your sweet light recede again?
I wake me in the dead of night,
  And start,--for through the misty gloom

Red Hecate stares--a boding sight!--
  Looks in, but never fills my room.

Thou music of my boyhood's hour!
  Thou shining light on manhood's way!
No more dost thou fair influence shower
  To move my soul by night or day.
O strange! that while in hall and street
  Thy hand I touch, thy grace I meet,
Such miles of polar ice should part
  The slightest touch of mind and heart!
But all thy love has waned, and so
  I gladly let thy beauty go.

Now that I am borrowing, I will also give a letter received at this time, and extracts from others from an earlier traveller, and in a different region of the country from that I saw, which, I think, in different ways, admirably descriptive of the country.

"And you, too, love the Prairies, flying voyager of a summer hour; but *I* have only there owned the wild forest, the wide-spread meadows; there only built my house, and seen the livelong day the thoughtful shadows of the great clouds color, with all-transient browns, the untrampled floor of grass; there has Spring pranked the long smooth reaches with those golden flowers, whereby became the fields a sea too golden to o'erlast the heats. Yes! and with many a yellow bell she gilded our unbounded path, that sank in the light swells of the varied surface, skirted the unfilled barrens, nor shunned the steep banks of rivers darting merrily on. There has the white snow frolicsomely strown itself, till all that vast, outstretched distance glittered like a mirror in which only the heavens were reflected, and among these drifts our steps have been curbed. Ah! many days of precious weather are on the Prairies!

"You have then found, after many a weary hour, when Time has locked your temples as in a circle of heated metal, some cool, sweet, swift-gliding moments, the iron ring of necessity ungirt, and the fevered pulses at rest. You have also found this where fresh nature suffers no ravage, amid those bowers of wild-wood, those dream-like, bee-sung, murmuring and musical plains, swimming under their hazy distances, as if there, in that warm and deep back ground, stood the fairy castle of our hopes, with its fountains, its pictures, its many mystical figures in repose. Ever could we rove over those sunny distances, breathing that modulated wind, eyeing those so well-blended, imaginative, yet thoughtful surfaces, and above us wide--wide a horizon effortless and superb as a young divinity.

"I was a prisoner where you glide, the summer's pensioned guest, and my chains were the past and the future, darkness and blowing sand. There, very weary, I received from the distance a sweet emblem of an incorruptible, lofty and pervasive nature, but was I less weary? I was a prisoner, and you, plains, were my prison bars.

"Yet never, O never, beautiful plains, had I any feeling for you but profoundest gratitude, for indeed ye are only fair, grand and majestic, while I had scarcely a right there. Now, ye stand in that past day, grateful images of unshattered repose, simple in your tranquillity, strong in your self-possession, yet ever musical and springing as the footsteps of a child.

"Ah! that to some poet, whose lyre had never lost a string, to whom mortality, kinder than is her custom, had vouchsafed a day whose down had been untouched,--that to him these plains might enter, and flow forth in airy song. And you, forests, under whose symmetrical shields of dark green the colors of the fawns move, like the waters of the river under its spears,--its cimeters of flag, where, in gleaming circles of steel, the breasts of the wood-pigeons flash in the playful sunbeam, and many sounds, many notes of no earthly music, come over the well-relieved glades,--should not your depth pass into that poet's heart,--in your depths should he not fuse his own?"

The other letters show the painter's eye, as this the poet's heart.

"Springfield, Illinois, May 20, 1840.
"Yesterday morning I left Griggsville, my knapsack at my back, pursued my journey all day on foot, and found so new and great delight in this charming country, that I must needs tell you about it. Do you remember our saying once, that we never found the trees tall enough, the fields green enough. Well, the trees are for

once tall, and fair to look upon, and one unvarying carpet of the tenderest green covers these marvellous fields, that spread out their smooth sod for miles and miles, till they even reach the horizon. But, to begin my day's journey. Griggsville is situated on the west side of the Illinois river, on a high prairie; between it and the river is a long range of bluffs which reaches a hundred miles north and south, then a wide river bottom, and then the river. It was a mild, showery morning, and I directed my steps toward the bluffs. They are covered with forest, not like our forests, tangled and impassable, but where the trees stand fair and apart from one another, so that you might ride every where about on horseback, and the tops of the hills are generally bald, and covered with green turf, like our pastures. Indeed, the whole country reminds me perpetually of one that has been carefully cultivated by a civilized people, who had been suddenly removed from the earth, with all the works of their hands, and the land given again into nature's keeping. The solitudes are not savage; they have not that dreary, stony loneliness that used to affect me in our own country; they never repel; there are no lonely heights, no isolated spots, but all is gentle, mild, inviting,--all is accessible. In following this winding, hilly road for four or five miles, I think I counted at least a dozen new kinds of wild flowers, not timid, retiring little plants like ours, but bold flowers of rich colors, covering the ground in abundance. One very common flower resembles our cardinal flower, though not of so deep a color, another is very like rocket or phlox, but smaller and of various colors, white, blue and purple. Beautiful white lupines I find too, violets white and purple. The vines and parasites are magnificent. I followed on this road till I came to the prairie which skirts the river, and this, of all the beauties of this region, is the most peculiar and wonderful. Imagine a vast and gently-swelling pasture of the brightest green grass, stretching away from you on every side, behind, toward these hills I have described, in all other directions, to a belt of tall trees, all growing up with noble proportions, from the generous soil. It is an unimagined picture of abundance and peace. Somewhere about, you are sure to see a huge herd, of cattle, often white, and generally brightly marked, grazing. All looks like the work of man's hand, but you see no vestige of man, save perhaps an almost imperceptible hut on the edge of the prairie. Reaching the river, I ferried myself across, and then crossed over to take the Jacksonville railroad, but, finding there was no train, passed the night at a farm house. And here may find its place this converse between the solitary old man and the young traveller.

SOLITARY.

My son, with weariness thou seemest spent,
And toiling on the dusty road all day,
Weary and pale, yet with inconstant step,
Hither and thither turning,--seekest thou
To find aught lost, or what dark care pursues thee?
If thou art weary, rest, if hungry, eat.

TRAVELLER.

Oh rather, father, let me ask of thee
What is it I do seek, what thing I lack?
These many days I've left my father's hall,
Forth driven by insatiable desire,
That, like the wind, now gently murmuring,
Enticed me forward with its own sweet voice
Through many-leaved woods, and valleys deep,
Yet ever fled before me. Then with sound
Stronger than hurrying tempest, seizing me,
Forced me to fly its power. Forward still,
Bound by enchanted ties, I seek its source.
Sometimes it is a something I have lost,
Known long since, before I bent my steps
Toward this beautiful broad plane of earth.
Sometimes it is a spirit yet unknown,
In whose dim-imaged features seem to smile
The dear delight of these high-mansioned thoughts,
That sometimes visit me. Like unto mine
Her lineaments appear, but beautiful,
As of a sister in a far-off world,

Waiting to welcome me. And when I think
To reach and clasp the figure, it is gone,
And some ill-omened ghastly vision comes
To bid beware, and not too curiously
Demand the secrets of that distant world,
Whose shadow haunts me.--On the waves below
But now I gazed, warmed with the setting sun,
Who sent his golden streamers to my feet,
It seemed a pathway to a world beyond,
And I looked round, if that my spirit beckoned
That I might follow it.

SOLITARY.

Dreams all, my son. Yes, even so I dreamed,
And even so was thwarted. You must learn
To dream another long and troublous dream.
The dream of life. And you shall think you wake,
And think the shadows substance, love and hate,
Exchange and barter, joy, and weep, and dance,
And this too shall be dream.

TRAVELLER.

Oh who can say
Where lies the boundary? What solid things
That daily mock our senses, shall dissolve
Before the might within, while shadowy forms
Freeze into stark reality, defying
The force and will of man. These forms I see,
They may go with me through eternity,
And bless or curse with ceaseless company,
While yonder man, that I met yesternight,

Where is he now? He passed before my eyes,
He is gone, but these stay with me ever.

That night the young man rested with the old,
And, grave or gay, in laughter or in tears,
They wore the night in converse. Morning came,
The dreamer took his solitary way;
And, as he pressed the old man's hand, he sighed,
Must this too be a dream?

Afterwards, of the rolling prairie. "There was one of twenty miles in extent, not flat, but high and rolling, so that when you arrived at a high part, by gentle ascents, the view was beyond measure grand; as far as the eye could reach, nothing but the green, rolling plain, and at a vast distance, groves, all looking gentle and cultivated, yet all uninhabited. I think it would impress you, as it does me, that these scenes are truly sublime. I have a sensation of vastness which I have sought in vain among high mountains. Mountains crowd one sensation on another, till all is excitement, all is surprise, wonder, enchantment. Here is neither enchantment or disappointment, but expectation fully realized. I have always had an attachment for a plain. The Roman Campagna is a prairie. Peoria is in a most lovely situation. In fact I am so delighted that I am as full of superlatives as the Italian language. I could, however, find fault enough, if you ask what I dislike."

But no one did ask; it is not worth while where there is so much to admire. Yet the following is a good statement of the shadow side.

"As to the boasts about the rapid progress here, give me rather the firm fibre of a slow and knotty growth. I could not help, thinking as much when I was talking to E. the other day, whom I met on board the boat. He quarrelled with Boston for its slowness; said it was a bad place for a young man. He could not make himself felt, could not see the effects of his exertions as he could here.--To be sure he could not. Here he comes, like a yankee farmer, with all the knowledge that our hard soil and laborious cultivation could give him, and what wonder if he is surprised at the work of his own hands, when he comes to such a soil as this. But he feeds not so many mouths, though he tills more acres. The plants he raises have not so exquisite a form, the vegetables so fine a flavor. His cultivation becomes more negligent, he is not so good a farmer. Is not this a true view? It strikes me continually. The traces of a man's hand in a new country are rarely productive of beauty. It is a cutting down of forest trees to make zigzag fences."

The most picturesque objects to be seen from Chicago on the inland side were the lines of Hoosier wagons. These rude farmers, the large first product of the soil, travel leisurely along, sleeping in their wagons by night, eating only what they bring with them. In the town they observe the same plan, and trouble no luxurious hotel for board and lodging. In the town they look like foreign peasantry, and contrast well with the many Germans, Dutch, and Irish. In the country it is very pretty to see them prepared to "camp out" at night, their horses taken out of harness, and they lounging under the trees, enjoying the evening meal.

On the lake side it is fine to see the great boats come panting it from their rapid and marvellous journey. Especially at night the motion of their lights is very majestic.

When the favorite boats, the Great Western and Illinois, are going out, the town is thronged with people from the south and farther west, to go in them. These moonlight nights I would hear the French rippling and fluttering familiarly amid the rude ups and downs of the Hoosier dialect.

At the hotel table were daily to be seen new faces, and new stories to be learned. And any one who has a large acquaintance may be pretty sure of meeting some of them here in the course of a few days.

Among those whom I met was Mrs. Z., the aunt of an old schoolmate, to whom I impatiently hastened, as soon as the meal was over, to demand news of Mariana. The answer startled me. Mariana, so full of life, was dead. That form, the most rich in energy and coloring of any I had ever seen, had faded from the earth. The circle of youthful associations had given way in the part, that seemed the strongest. What I now learned of the story of this life, and what was by myself remembered, may be bound together in this slight sketch.

At the boarding-school to which I was too early sent, a fond, a proud, and timid child, I saw among the ranks of the gay and graceful, bright or earnest girls, only one who interested my fancy or touched my young heart; and this was Mariana. She was, on the father's side, of Spanish Creole blood, but had been sent to the Atlantic coast, to receive a school education under the care of her aunt, Mrs. Z.

This lady had kept her mostly at home with herself, and Mariana had gone from her house to a day-school; but the aunt, being absent for a time in Europe, she had now been unfortunately committed for some time to the mercies of a boarding-school.

A strange bird she proved there,--a lonely swallow that could not make for itself a summer. At first, her schoolmates were captivated with her ways; her love of wild dances and sudden song, her freaks of passion and of wit. She was always new, always surprising, and, for a time, charming.

But, after awhile, they tired of her. She could never be depended on to join in their plans, yet she expected them to follow out hers with their whole strength. She was very loving, even infatuated in her own affections, and exacted from those who had professed any love for her, the devotion she was willing to bestow.

Yet there was a vein of haughty caprice in her character; a love of solitude, which made her at times wish to retire entirely, and at these times she would expect to be thoroughly understood, and let alone, yet to be welcomed back when she returned. She did not thwart others in their humors, but she never doubted of great indulgence from them.

Some singular habits she had which, when new, charmed, but, after acquaintance, displeased her companions. She had by nature the same habit and power of excitement that is described in the spinning dervishes of the East. Like them, she would spin until all around her were giddy, while her own brain, instead of being disturbed, was excited to great action. Pausing, she would declaim verse of others or her own; act many parts, with strange catch-words and burdens that seemed to act with mystical power on her own fancy, sometimes stimulating her to convulse the hearer with laughter, sometimes to melt him to tears. When her power began to languish, she would spin again till fired to recommence her singular drama, into which she wove figures from the scenes of her earlier childhood, her companions, and the dignitaries she sometimes saw, with fantasies unknown to life, unknown to heaven or earth.

This excitement, as may be supposed, was not good for her. It oftenest came on in the evening, and often spoiled her sleep. She would wake in the night, and cheat her restlessness by inventions that teazed, while they sometimes diverted her companions.

She was also a sleep-walker; and this one trait of her case did somewhat alarm her guardians, who, otherwise, showed the same profound stupidity as to this peculiar being, usual in the overseers of the young. They consulted a physician, who said she would outgrow it, and prescribed a milk diet.

Meantime, the fever of this ardent and too early stimulated nature was constantly increased by the restraints and narrow routine of the boarding school. She was always devising means to break in upon it. She had a taste which would have seemed ludicrous to her mates, if they had not felt some awe of her, from a touch of genius and power that never left her, for costume and fancy dresses, always some sash twisted about her, some drapery, something odd in the arrangement of her hair and dress, so that the methodical preceptress dared not let her go out without a careful scrutiny and remodelling, whose soberizing effects generally disappeared the moment she was in the free air.

At last, a vent for her was found in private theatricals. Play followed play, and in these and the rehearsals she found entertainment congenial with her. The principal parts, as a matter of course, fell to her lot; most of the good suggestions and arrangements came from her, and for a time she ruled masterly and shone triumphant.

During these performances the girls had heightened their natural bloom with artificial red; this was delightful to them--it was something so out of the way. But Mariana, after the plays were over, kept her carmine saucer on the dressing-table, and put on her blushes regularly as the morning.

When stared and jeered at, she at first said she did it because she thought it made her look prettier; but, after a while, she became quite petulant about it,-- would make no reply to any joke, but merely kept on doing it.

This irritated the girls, as all eccentricity does the world in general, more than vice or malignity. They talked it over among themselves, till they got wrought up to a desire of punishing, once for all, this sometimes amusing, but so often provoking nonconformist.

Having obtained the leave of the mistress, they laid, with great glee, a plan one evening, which was to be carried into execution next day at dinner.

Among Mariana's irregularities was a great aversion to the meal-time ceremonial. So long, so tiresome she found it, to be seated at a certain moment, to wait while each one was served at so large a table, and one where there was scarcely any conversation; from day to day it became more heavy to her to sit there, or go there at all. Often as possible she excused herself on the ever-convenient plea of headache, and was hardly ever ready when the dinner-bell rang.

To-day it found her on the balcony, lost in gazing on the beautiful prospect. I have heard her say afterwards, she had rarely in her life been so happy,--and she was one with whom happiness was a still rapture. It was one of the most blessed summer days; the shadows of great white clouds empurpled the distant hills for a few moments only to leave them more golden; the tall grass of the wide fields waved in the softest breeze. Pure blue were the heavens, and the same hue of pure contentment was in the heart of Mariana.

Suddenly on her bright mood jarred the dinner bell. At first rose her usual thought, I will not, cannot go; and then the ***must***, which daily life can always enforce, even upon the butterflies and birds, came, and she walked reluctantly to her room. She merely changed her dress, and never thought of adding the artificial rose to her cheek.

When she took her seat in the dining-hall, and was asked if she would be helped, raising her eyes, she saw the person who asked her was deeply rouged, with a bright glaring spot, perfectly round, in either cheek. She looked at the next, same apparition! She then slowly passed her eyes down the whole line, and saw the same, with a suppressed smile distorting every countenance. Catching the design at once, she deliberately looked along her own side of the table, at every schoolmate in turn; every one had joined in the trick. The teachers strove to be grave, but she saw they enjoyed the joke. The servants could not suppress a titter.

When Warren Hastings stood at the bar of Westminster Hall--when the Methodist preacher walked through a line of men, each of whom greeted him with a brickbat or a rotten egg, they had some preparation for the crisis, and it might not be very difficult to meet it with an impassive brow. Our little girl was quite unprepared to find herself in the midst of a world which despised her, and triumphed in her disgrace.

She had ruled, like a queen, in the midst of her companions; she had shed her animation through their lives, and loaded them with prodigal favors, nor once suspected that a powerful favorite might not be loved. Now, she felt that she had been but a dangerous plaything in the hands of those whose hearts she never had doubted.

Yet, the occasion found her equal to it, for Mariana had the kind of spirit, which, in a better cause, had made the Roman matron truly say of her death-wound, "It is not painful, Poetus." She did not blench--she did not change countenance. She swallowed her dinner with apparent composure. She made remarks to those near her, as if she had no eyes.

The wrath of the foe of course rose higher, and the moment they were freed from the restraints of the dining-room, they all ran off, gaily calling, and sarcastically laughing, with backward glances, at Mariana, left alone.

She went alone to her room, locked the door, and threw herself on the floor in strong convulsions. These had sometimes threatened her life, as a child, but of later years, she had outgrown them. School-hours came, and she was not there. A little girl, sent to her door, could get no answer. The teachers became alarmed, and broke it open. Bitter was their penitence and that of her companions at the state in which they found her. For some hours, terrible anxiety was felt; but, at last, nature, exhausted, relieved herself by a deep slumber.

From this Mariana rose an altered being. She made no reply to the expressions of sorrow from her companions, none to the grave and kind, but undiscerning comments of her teacher. She did not name the source of her anguish, and its poisoned dart sank deeply in. It was this thought which stung her so. What, not one, not a single one, in the hour of trial, to take my part, not one who refused to take part against me. Past words of love, and caresses, little heeded at the time, rose to her memory, and gave fuel to her distempered thoughts. Beyond the sense of universal perfidy, of burning resentment, she could not get. And Mariana, born for love, now hated all the world.

The change, however, which these feelings made in her conduct and appearance bore no such construction to the careless observer. Her gay freaks were quite gone, her wildness, her invention. Her dress was uniform, her manner much subdued. Her chief interest seemed now to lie in her studies, and in music. Her companions she never sought, but they, partly from uneasy remorseful feelings, partly that they really liked her much better now that she did not oppress and puzzle them, sought her continually. And here the black shadow comes upon her life, the only stain upon the history of Mariana.

They talked to her, as girls, having few topics, naturally do, of one another. And the demon rose within her, and spontaneously, without design, generally without words of positive falsehood, she became a genius of discord among them. She fanned those flames of envy and jealousy which a wise, true word from a third will often quench forever; by a glance, or a seemingly light reply, she planted the seeds of dissension, till there was scarce a peaceful affection, or sincere intimacy in the circle where she lived, and could not but rule, for she was one whose nature was to that of the others as fire to clay.

It was at this time that I came to the school, and first saw Mariana. Me she charmed at once, for I was a sentimental child, who, in my early ill health, had been indulged in reading novels, till I had no eyes for the common greens and browns of life. The heroine of one of these, "The Bandit's Bride," I immediately saw in Mariana. Surely the Bandit's Bride had just such hair, and such strange, lively ways, and such a sudden flash of the eye. The Bandit's Bride, too, was born to be "misunderstood" by all but her lover. But Mariana, I was determined, should be more fortunate, for, until her lover appeared, I myself would be the wise and delicate being who could understand her.

It was not, however, easy to approach her for this purpose. Did I offer to run and fetch her handkerchief, she was obliged to go to her room, and would rather do it herself. She did not like to have people turn over for her the leaves of the music book as she played. Did I approach my stool to her feet, she moved away, as if to give me room. The bunch of wild flowers which I timidly laid beside her plate was left there.

After some weeks my desire to attract her notice really preyed upon me, and one day meeting her alone in the entry, I fell upon my knees, and kissing her hand, cried, "O Mariana, do let me love you, and try to love me a little." But my idol snatched away her hand, and, laughing more wildly than the Bandit's Bride was ever described to have done, ran into her room. After that day her manner to me was not only cold, but repulsive; I felt myself scorned, and became very unhappy.

Perhaps four months had passed thus, when, one afternoon, it became obvious that something more than common was brewing. Dismay and mystery were written in many faces of the older girls; much whispering was going on in corners.

In the evening, after prayers, the principal bade us stay; and, in a grave, sad voice, summoned forth Mariana to answer charges to be made against her.

Mariana came forward, and leaned against the chimney-piece. Eight of the older girls came forward, and preferred against her charges, alas, too well-founded, of calumny and falsehood.

My heart sank within me, as one after the other brought up their proofs, and I saw they were too strong to be resisted. I could not bear the thought of this second disgrace of my shining favorite. The first had been whispered to me, though the girls did not like to talk about it. I must confess, such is the charm of strength to softer natures, that neither of these crises could deprive Mariana of hers in my eyes.

At first, she defended herself with self-possession and eloquence. But when she found she could no more resist the truth, she suddenly threw herself down, dashing her head, with all her force, against the iron hearth, on which a fire was burning, and was taken up senseless.

The affright of those present was great. Now that they had perhaps killed her, they reflected it would have been as well, if they had taken warning from the former occasion, and approached very carefully a nature so capable of any extreme. After awhile she revived, with a faint groan, amid the sobs of her companions. I was on my knees by the bed, and held her cold hand. One of those most aggrieved took it from me to beg her pardon, and say it was impossible not to love her. She made no reply.

Neither that night, nor for several days, could a word be obtained from her, nor would she touch food; but, when it was presented to her, or any one drew near for any cause, she merely turned away her head, and gave no sign. The teacher saw that some terrible nervous affection had fallen upon her, that she grew more and more feverish. She knew not what to do.

Meanwhile a new revolution had taken place in the mind of the passionate, but nobly-tempered child. All these months nothing but the sense of injury had rankled in her heart. She had gone on in one mood, doing what the demon prompted, without scruple and without fear.

But, at the moment of detection, the tide ebbed, and the bottom of her soul lay revealed to her eye. How black, how stained and sad. Strange, strange that she had not seen before the baseness and cruelty of falsehood, the loveliness of truth. Now, amid the wreck, uprose the moral nature which never before had attained the ascendant. "But," she thought, "too late, sin is revealed to me in all its deformity, and, sin-defiled, I will not, cannot live. The, mainspring of life is broken."

And thus passed slowly by her hours in that black despair of which only youth is capable. In older years men suffer more dull pain, as each sorrow that comes drops its leaden weight into the past, and, similar features of character bringing similar results, draws up a heavy burden buried in those depths. But only youth has energy, with fixed unwinking gaze, to contemplate grief, to hold it in the arms and to the heart, like a child which makes it wretched, yet is indubitably its own.

The lady who took charge of this sad child had never well understood her before, but had always looked on her with great tenderness. And now love seemed, when all around were in greatest distress, fearing to call in medical aid, fearing to do without it, to teach her where the only balm was to be found that could have healed this wounded spirit.

One night she came in, bringing a calming draught. Mariana was sitting, as usual, her hair loose, her dress the same robe they had put on her at first, her eyes fixed vacantly upon the whited wall. To the proffers and entreaties of her nurse she made no reply.

The lady burst into tears, but Mariana did not seem even to observe it.

The lady then said, "O my child, do not despair, do not think that one great fault can mar a whole life. Let me trust you, let me tell you the griefs of my sad life. I will tell to you, Mariana, what I never expected to impart to any one."

And so she told her tale: it was one of pain, of shame, borne, not for herself, but for one near and dear as herself. Mariana knew the lady, knew the pride and reserve of her nature; she had often admired to see how the cheek, lovely, but no longer young, mantled with the deepest blush of youth, and the blue eyes were cast down at any little emotion. She had understood the proud sensibility of the character. She fixed her eyes on those now raised to hers, bright with fast falling tears. She heard the story to the end, and then, without saying a word, stretched out her hand for the cup.

She returned to life, but it was as one who has passed through the valley of death. The heart of stone was quite broken in her. The fiery life fallen from flame to coal. When her strength was a little restored, she had all her companions summoned, and said to them; "I deserved to die, but a generous trust has called me back to life. I will be worthy of it, nor ever betray the truth, or resent injury more. Can you forgive the past?"

And they not only forgave, but, with love and earnest tears, clasped in their arms the returning sister. They vied with one another in offices of humble love to the humbled one; and, let it be recorded as an instance of the pure honor of which young hearts are capable, that these facts, known to forty persons, never, so far as I know, transpired beyond those walls.

It was not long after this that Mariana was summoned home. She went thither a wonderfully instructed being, though in ways those who had sent her forth to learn little dreamed of.

Never was forgotten the vow of the returning prodigal. Mariana could not resent, could not play false. The terrible crisis, which she so early passed through, probably prevented the world from hearing much of her. A wild fire was tamed in that hour of penitence at the boarding school, such as has oftentimes wrapped court and camp in its destructive glow.

But great were the perils she had yet to undergo, for she was one of those barks which easily get beyond soundings, and ride not lightly on the plunging billow.

Her return to her native climate seconded the effects of inward revolutions. The cool airs of the north had exasperated nerves too susceptible for their tension. Those of the south restored her to a more soft and indolent state. Energy gave place to feeling, turbulence to intensity of character.

At this time love was the natural guest, and he came to her under a form that might have deluded one less ready for delusion.

Sylvain was a person well proportioned to her lot in years, family, and fortune. His personal beauty was not great, but of a noble character. Repose marked his slow gesture, and the steady gaze of his large brown eye, but it was a repose that would give way to a blaze of energy when the occasion called. In his stature, expression, and heavy coloring, he might not unfitly be represented by the great magnolias that inhabit the forests of that climate. His voice, like everything about him, was rich and soft, rather than sweet or delicate.

Mariana no sooner knew him than she loved, and her love, lovely as she was, soon excited his. But, oh! it is a curse to woman to love first, or most. In so doing she reverses the natural relations, and her heart can never, never be satisfied with what ensues.

Mariana loved first, and loved most, for she had most force and variety to love with. Sylvain seemed, at first, to take her to himself, as the deep southern night might some fair star. But it proved not so.

Mariana was a very intellectual being, and she needed companionship. This she could only have with Sylvain, in the paths of passion and action. Thoughts he had none, and little delicacy of sentiment. The gifts she loved to prepare of such for him, he took with a sweet, but indolent smile; he held them lightly, and soon they fell from his grasp. He loved to have her near him, to feel the glow and fragrance of her nature, but cared not to explore the little secret paths whence that fragrance was collected.

Mariana knew not this for a long time. Loving so much, she imagined all the rest, and, where she felt a blank, always hoped that further communion would fill it up. When she found this could never be; that there was absolutely a whole province of her being to which nothing in his answered, she was too deeply in love to leave him. Often after passing hours together, beneath the southern moon, when, amid the sweet intoxication of mutual love, she still felt the desolation of solitude, and a repression of her finer powers, she had asked herself, can I give him up? But the heart always passionately answered, no! I may be miserable with him, but I cannot live without him.

And the last miserable feeling of these conflicts was, that if the lover, soon to be the bosom friend, could have dreamed of these conflicts, he would have laughed, or else been angry, even enough to give her up.

Ah weakness of the strong. Of these strong only where strength is weakness. Like others she had the decisions of life to make, before she had light by which to make them. Let none condemn her. Those who have not erred as fatally, should thank the guardian angel who gave them more time to prepare for judgment, but blame no children who thought at arm's length to find the moon. Mariana, with a heart capable of highest Eros, gave it to one who knew love only as a flower or plaything, and bound her heartstrings to one who parted his as lightly as the ripe fruit leaves the bough. The sequel could not fail. Many console themselves for the one great mistake with their children, with the world. This was not possible to Mariana. A few months of domestic life she still was almost happy. But Sylvain then grew tired. He wanted business and the world; of these she had no knowledge, for them no faculties. He wanted in her the head of his house; she to make her heart his home. No compromise was possible between natures of such unequal poise, and which had met only on one or two points. Through all its stages she

> "felt
> The agonizing sense
> Of seeing lore from passion melt
> Into indifference;
> The fearful shame that, day by day,
> Burns onward, still to burn,
> To have thrown her precious heart away,
> And met this black return,"

till death at last closed the scene. Not that she died of one downright blow on the heart. That is not the way such cases proceed. I cannot detail all the symptoms, for I was not there to watch them, and aunt Z. was neither so faithful an observer or narrator as I have shown myself in the school-day passages; but, generally, they were as follows.

Sylvain wanted to go into the world, or let it into his house. Mariana consented; but, with an unsatisfied heart, and no lightness of character, she played her part ill there. The sort of talent and facility she had displayed in early days, were not the least like what is called out in the social world by the desire to please and to shine. Her excitement had been muse-like, that of the improvisatrice, whose kindling fancy seeks to create an atmosphere round it, and makes the chain through which to set free its electric sparks. That had been a time of wild and exuberant life. After her character became more tender and concentrated, strong affection or a pure enthusiasm might still have called out beautiful talents in her. But in the first she was utterly disappointed. The second was not roused within her thought. She did not expand into various life, and remained unequal; sometimes too passive, sometimes too ardent, and not sufficiently occupied with what occupied those around her to come on the same level with them and embellish their hours.

Thus she lost ground daily with her husband, who, comparing her with the careless shining dames of society, wondered why he had found her so charming in solitude.

At intervals, when they were left alone, Mariana wanted to open her heart, to tell the thoughts of her mind. She was so conscious of secret riches within herself, that sometimes it seemed, could she but reveal a glimpse of them to the eye of Sylvain, he would be attracted near her again, and take a path where they could walk hand in hand. Sylvain, in these intervals, wanted an indolent repose. His home was his castle. He wanted no scenes too exciting there. Light jousts and plays were well enough, but no grave encounters. He liked to lounge, to sing, to read, to sleep. In fine, Sylvain became the kind, but preoccupied husband, Mariana, the solitary and wretched wife. He was off continually, with his male companions, on excursions or affairs of pleasure. At home Mariana found that neither her books nor music would console her.

She was of too strong a nature to yield without a struggle to so dull a fiend as despair. She looked into other hearts, seeking whether she could there find such home as an orphan asylum may afford. This she did rather because the chance came to her, and it seemed unfit not to seize the proffered plank, than in hope, for she was not one to double her stakes, but rather with Cassandra power to discern early the sure course of the game. And Cassandra whispered that she was one of those

"Whom men love not, but yet regret."

And so it proved. Just as in her childish days, though in a different form, it happened betwixt her and these companions. She could not be content to receive them quietly, but was stimulated to throw herself too much into the tie, into the hour, till she filled it too full for them. Like Fortunio, who sought to do homage to his friends by building a fire of cinnamon, not knowing that its perfume would be too strong for their endurance, so did Mariana. What she wanted to tell, they did not wish to hear; a little had pleased, so much overpowered, and they preferred the free air of the street, even, to the cinnamon perfume of her palace.

However, this did not signify; had they staid, it would not have availed her! It was a nobler road, a higher aim she needed now; this did not become clear to her.

She lost her appetite, she fell sick, had fever. Sylvain was alarmed, nursed her tenderly; she grew better. Then his care ceased, he saw not the mind's disease, but left her to rise into health and recover the tone of her spirits, as she might. More solitary than ever, she tried to raise herself, but she knew not yet enough. The weight laid upon her young life was a little too heavy for it. One long day she passed alone, and the thoughts and presages came too thick for her strength. She knew not what to do with them, relapsed into fever, and died.

Notwithstanding this weakness, I must ever think of her as a fine sample of womanhood, born to shed light and life on some palace home. Had she known more of God and the universe, she would not have given way where so many have conquered. But peace be with her; she now, perhaps, has entered into a larger freedom, which is knowledge. With her died a great interest in life to me. Since her I have never seen a Bandit's Bride. She, indeed, turned out to be only a merchant's.--Sylvain is married again to a fair and laughing girl, who will not die, probably, till their marriage grows a "golden marriage."

Aunt Z. had with her some papers of Mariana's, which faintly shadow forth the thoughts that engaged her in the last days. One of these seems to have been written when some faint gleam had been thrown across the path, only to make its darkness more visible. It seems to have been suggested by remembrance of the beautiful ballad, **Helen of Kirconnel Lee**, which once she loved to recite, and in tones that would not have sent a chill to the heart from which it came.

> "Death
> Opens her sweet white arms, and whispers Peace;
> Come, say thy sorrows in this bosom! This
> Will never close against thee, and my heart,
> Though cold, cannot be colder much than man's."

> "I wish I were where Helen lies,"
> A lover in the times of old,
> Thus vents his grief in lonely sighs,
> And hot tears from a bosom cold.

But, mourner for thy martyred love,
Could'st thou but know what hearts must feel,
  Where no sweet recollections move,
Whose tears a desert fount reveal.

  When "in thy arms burd Helen fell,"
She died, sad man, she died for thee,
  Nor could the films of death dispel
Her loving eye's sweet radiancy.

  Thou wert beloved, and she had loved,
Till death alone the whole could tell,
  Death every shade of doubt removed,
And steeped the star in its cold well.

  On some fond breast the parting soul
Relies,--earth has no more to give;
  Who wholly loves has known the whole,
The wholly loved doth truly live.

  But some, sad outcasts from this prize,
Wither down to a lonely grave,
  All hearts their hidden love despise,
And leave them to the whelming wave.

  They heart to heart have never pressed,
Nor hands in holy pledge have given,
  By father's love were ne'er caressed,
Nor in a mother's eye saw heaven.

  A flowerless and fruitless tree,
A dried up stream, a mateless bird,
  They live, yet never living be,

They die, their music all unheard.

  I wish I were where Helen lies,
For there I could not be alone;
  But now, when this dull body dies,
The spirit still will make its moan.

  Love passed me by, nor touched my brow;
Life would not yield one perfect boon;
  And all too late it calls me now,
O all too late, and all too soon.

  If thou couldst the dark riddle read
Which leaves this dart within my breast,
  Then might I think thou lov'st indeed,
Then were the whole to thee confest.

  Father, they will not take me home,
To the poor child no heart is free;
  In sleet and snow all night I roam;
Father,--was this decreed by thee?

  I will not try another door,
To seek what I have never found;
  Now, till the very last is o'er,
Upon the earth I'll wander round.

  I will not hear the treacherous call
That bids me stay and rest awhile,
  For I have found that, one and all,
They seek me for a prey and spoil.

> They are not bad, I know it well;
> I know they know not what they do;
>   They are the tools of the dread spell
> Which the lost lover must pursue.
>
>   In temples sometimes she may rest,
> In lonely groves, away from men,
>   There bend the head, by heats distrest,
> Nor be by blows awoke again.
>
>   Nature is kind, and God is kind,
> And, if she had not had a heart,
>   Only that great discerning mind,
> She might have acted well her part.
>
>   But oh this thirst, that none can still,
> Save those unfounden waters free;
>   The angel of my life should fill
> And soothe me to Eternity!

It marks the defect in the position of woman that one like Mariana should have found reason to write thus. To a man of equal power, equal sincerity, no more!-- many resources would have presented themselves. He would not have needed to seek, he would have been called by life, and not permitted to be quite wrecked through the affections only. But such women as Mariana are often lost, unless they meet some man of sufficiently great soul to prize them.

Van Artevelde's Elena, though in her individual nature unlike my Mariana, is like her in a mind whose large impulses are disproportioned to the persons and occasions she meets, and which carry her beyond those reserves which mark the appointed lot of woman. But, when she met Van Artevelde, he was too great not to revere her rare nature, without regard to the stains and errors of its past history; great enough to receive her entirely and make a new life for her; man enough to be a lover! But as such men come not so often as once an age, their presence should not be absolutely needed to sustain life.

At Chicago I read again Philip Van Artevelde, and certain passages in it will always be in my mind associated with the deep sound of the lake, as heard in the night. I used to read a short time at night, and then open the blind to look out. The moon would be full upon the lake, and the calm breath, pure light, and the deep voice harmonized well with the thought of the Flemish hero. When will this country have such a man? It is what she needs; no thin Idealist, no coarse Realist, but a man whose eye reads the heavens while his feet step firmly on the ground, and his hands are strong and dexterous for the use of human implements. A man religious, virtuous and--sagacious; a man of universal sympathies, but self-possessed; a man who knows the region of emotion, though he is not its slave; a man to whom this world is no mere spectacle, or fleeting shadow, but a great solemn game to be played with good heed, for its stakes are of eternal value, yet who, if his own play be true, heeds not what he loses by the falsehood of others. A man who hives from the past, yet knows that its honey can but moderately avail him; whose comprehensive eye scans the present, neither infatuated by its golden lures, nor chilled by its many ventures; who possesses prescience, as the wise man must, but not so far as to be driven mad to-day by the gift which discerns to-morrow. When there is such a man for America, the thought which urges her on will be expressed.

Now that I am about to leave Illinois, feelings of regret and admiration come over me, as in parting with a friend whom we have not had the good sense to prize and study, while hours of association, never perhaps to return, were granted. I have fixed my attention almost exclusively on the picturesque beauty of this region; it was so new, so inspiring. But I ought to have been more interested in the housekeeping of this magnificent state, in the education she is giving her children, in their prospects.

Illinois is, at present, a by-word of reproach among the nations, for the careless, prodigal course, by which, in early youth, she has endangered her honor. But you cannot look about you there, without seeing that there are resources abundant to retrieve, and soon to retrieve, far greater errors, if they are only directed with wisdom.

Might the simple maxim, that honesty is the best policy be laid to heart! Might a sense of the true aims of life elevate the tone of politics and trade, till public and private honor become identical! Might the western man in that crowded and exciting life which develops his faculties so fully for to-day, not forget that better part which could not be taken from him! Might the western woman take that interest and acquire that light for the education of the children, for which she alone has leisure!

This is indeed the great problem of the place and time. If the next generation be well prepared for their work, ambitious of good and skilful to achieve it, the children of the present settlers may be leaven enough for the mass constantly increasing by emigration. And how much is this needed where those rude foreigners can so little understand the best interests of the land they seek for bread and shelter. It would be a happiness to aid in this good work, and interweave the white and golden threads into the fate of Illinois. It would be a work worthy the devotion of any mind.

In the little that I saw, was a large proportion of intelligence, activity, and kind feeling; but, if there was much serious laying to heart of the true purposes of life, it did not appear in the tone of conversation.

Having before me the Illinois guide-book, I find there mentioned, as a "visionary," one of the men I should think of as able to be a truly valuable settler in a new and great country--Morris Birkbeck, of England. Since my return, I have read his journey to, and letters from, Illinois. I see nothing promised there that will not surely belong to the man who knows how to seek for it.

Mr. Birkbeck was an enlightened philanthropist, the rather that he did not wish to sacrifice himself to his fellow men, but to benefit them with all he had, and was, and wished. He thought all the creatures of a divine love ought to be happy and ought to be good, and that his own soul and his own life were not less precious than those of others; indeed, that to keep these healthy, was his only means of a healthy influence.

But his aims were altogether generous. Freedom, the liberty of law, not license; not indolence, work for himself and children, and all men, but under genial and poetic influences;--these were his aims. How different from those of the new settlers in general! And into his mind so long ago shone steadily the two thoughts, now so prevalent in thinking and aspiring minds, of "Resist not evil," and "Every man his own priest, and the heart the only true church."

He has lost credit for sagacity from accidental circumstances. It does not appear that his position was ill chosen, or his means disproportioned to his ends, had he been sustained by funds from England, as he had a right to expect. But through the profligacy of a near relative, commissioned to collect these dues, he was disappointed of them, and his paper protested and credit destroyed in our cities, before he became aware of his danger.

Still, though more slowly and with more difficulty, he might have succeeded in his designs. The English farmer might have made the English settlement a model for good methods and good aims to all that region, had not death prematurely cut short his plans.

I have wished to say these few words, because the veneration with which I have been inspired for his character by those who knew him well, makes me impatient of this careless blame being passed from mouth to mouth and book, to book. Success is no test of a man's endeavor, and Illinois will yet, I hope, regard this man, who knew so well what ***ought*** to be, as one of her true patriarchs, the Abraham of a promised land.

He was one too much before his time to be soon valued; but the time is growing up to him, and will understand his mild philanthropy and clear, large views.

I subjoin the account of his death, given me by a friend, as expressing, in fair picture, the character of the man.

"Mr. Birkbeck was returning from the seat of government, whither he had been on public business, and was accompanied by his son Bradford, a youth of sixteen or eighteen. It was necessary to cross a ford, which was rendered difficult by the swelling of the stream. Mr. B.'s horse was unwilling to plunge into the water, so his son offered to go first, and he followed. Bradford's horse had just gained footing on the opposite shore, when he looked back and perceived his father was dismounted, struggling in the water, and carried down by the current.

"Mr. Birkbeck could not swim; Bradford could; so he dismounted, and plunged into the stream to save his father. He got to him before he sank, held him up above water, and told him to take hold of his collar, and he would swim ashore with him. Mr. B. did so, and Bradford exerted all his strength to stem the current and reach the shore at a point where they could land; but, encumbered by his own clothing and his father's weight, he made no progress; and when Mr. B. perceived this, he, with his characteristic calmness and resolution, gave up his hold of his son, and, motioning to him to save himself, resigned himself to his fate. His son reached the shore, but was too much overwhelmed by his loss to leave it. He was found by some travellers, many hours after, seated on the margin of the stream, with his head in his hands, stupefied with grief.

"The body was found, and on the countenance was the sweetest smile; and Bradford said, 'just so he smiled upon me when he let go and pushed me away from him.'"

Many men can choose the right and best on a great occasion, but not many can, with such ready and serene decision, lay aside even life, when it is right and best. This little narrative touched my imagination in very early youth, and often has come up, in lonely vision, that face, serenely smiling above the current which bore him away to another realm of being.

CHAPTER V.
WISCONSIN.

A territory, not yet a state; still, nearer the acorn than we were.

It was very pleasant coming up. These large and elegant boats are so well arranged that every excursion may be a party of pleasure. There are many fair shows to see on the lake and its shores, almost always new and agreeable persons on board, pretty children playing about, ladies singing, (and if not very well, there is room to keep out of the way.) You may see a great deal here of Life, in the London sense, if you know a few people; or if you do not, and have the tact to look about you without seeming to stare.

We came to Milwaukie, where we were to pass a fortnight or more.

This place is most beautifully situated. A little river, with romantic banks, passes up through the town. The bank of the lake is here a bold bluff, eighty feet in height. From its summit, you enjoyed a noble outlook on the lake. A little narrow path wound along the edge of the lake below. I liked this walk much. Above me this high wall of rich earth, garlanded on its crest with trees, the long ripples of the lake coming up to my feet. Here, standing in the shadow, I could appreciate better its magnificent changes of color, which are the chief beauties of the lake-waters; but these are indescribable.

It was fine to ascend into the lighthouse, above this bluff, and watch from thence the thunder-clouds which so frequently rose over the lake, or the great boats coming in. Approaching the Milwaukie pier, they made a bend, and seemed to do obeisance in the heavy style of some dowager duchess entering a circle she wishes to treat with especial respect.

These boats come in and out every day, and still afford a cause for general excitement. The people swarm down to greet them, to receive and send away their packages and letters. To me they seemed such mighty messengers, to give, by their noble motion, such an idea of the power and fullness of life, that they were worthy to carry despatches from king to king. It must be very pleasant for those who have an active share in carrying on the affairs of this great and growing world to see them come in. It must be very pleasant to those who have dearly loved friends at the next station. To those who have neither business nor friends, it sometimes gives a desolating sense of insignificance.

The town promises to be, some time, a fine one, as it is so well situated; and they have good building material--a yellow brick, very pleasing to the eye. It seems to grow before you, and has indeed but just emerged from the thickets of oak and wild roses. A few steps will take you into the thickets, and certainly I never saw so many wild roses, or of so beautiful a red. Of such a color were the first red ones the world ever saw, when, says the legend, Venus flying to the assistance of Adonis, the rosebushes kept catching her to make her stay, and the drops of blood the thorns drew from her feet, as she tore herself away, fell on the white roses, and turned them this beautiful red.

I will here insert, though with no excuse, except that it came to memory at the time, this description of Titian's Venus and Adonis.

"This picture has that perfect balance of lines and forms that it would, (as was said of all Raphael's) 'seen at any distance have the air of an ornamental design.' It also tolls its story at the first glance, though, like all beautiful works, it gains by study.

"On one side slumbers the little God of Love, as an emblem, I suppose, that only the love of man is worth embodying, for surely Cytherea's is awake enough. The quiver of Cupid, suspended to a tree, gives sportive grace to the scene which softens the tragedy of a breaking tie. The dogs of Adonis pull upon his hand; he can scarce forbear to burst from the detaining arms of Beauty herself, yet he waits a moment to coax her--to make an unmeaning promise. 'A moment, a moment, my love, and I will return; a moment only.' Adonis is not beautiful, except in his expression of eager youth. The Queen of Beauty does not choose Apollo. Venus herself is very beautiful; especially the body is lovely as can be; and the soft, imploring look, gives a conjugal delicacy to the face which purifies the whole picture. This Venus is not as fresh, as moving and breathing as Shakspeare's, yet lovelier to the mind if not to the sense. 'T is difficult to look at this picture without indignation, because it is, in one respect, so true. Why must women always try to detain and restrain what they love? Foolish beauty; let him go; it is thy tenderness that has spoiled him. Be less lovely--less feminine; abandon thy fancy for giving thyself wholly; cease to love so well, and any Hercules will spin among thy maids, if thou wilt. But let him go this time; thou canst not keep him. Sit there, by thyself, on that bank, and, instead of thinking how soon he will come back, think how thou may'st love him no better than he does thee, for the time has come."

It was soon after this moment that the poor Queen, hearing the frightened hounds, apprehended the rash huntsman's danger, and, flying through the woods, gave their hue to the red roses.

To return from the Grecian isles to Milwaukie. One day, walking along the river's bank in search of a waterfall to be seen from one ravine, we heard tones from a band of music, and saw a gay troop shooting at a mark, on the opposite bank. Between every shot the band played; the effect was very pretty.

On this walk we found two of the oldest and most gnarled hemlocks that ever afforded study for a painter. They were the only ones we saw; they seemed the veterans of a former race.

At Milwaukie, as at Chicago, are many pleasant people, drawn together from all parts of the world. A resident here would find great piquancy in the associations,--those he met having such dissimilar histories and topics. And several persons I saw evidently transplanted from the most refined circles to be met in this country. There are lures enough in the West for people of all kinds;--the enthusiast and the cunning man; the naturalist, and the lover who needs to be rich for the sake of her he loves.

The torrent of emigration swells very strongly towards this place. During the fine weather, the poor refugees arrive daily, in their national dresses, all travel-soiled and worn. The night they pass in rude shantees, in a particular quarter of the town, then walk off into the country--the mothers carrying their infants, the fathers leading the little children by the hand, seeking a home, where their hands may maintain them.

One morning we set off in their track, and travelled a day's journey into this country,--fair, yet not, in that part which I saw, comparable, in my eyes, to the

Rock River region. It alternates rich fields, proper for grain, with oak openings, as they are called; bold, various and beautiful were the features of the scene, but I saw not those majestic sweeps, those boundless distances, those heavenly fields; it was not the same world.

Neither did we travel in the same delightful manner. We were now in a nice carriage, which must not go off the road, for fear of breakage, with a regular coachman, whose chief care was not to tire his horses, and who had no taste for entering fields in pursuit of wild flowers, or tempting some strange wood path in search of whatever might befall. It was pleasant, but almost as tame as New England.

But charming indeed was the place where we stopped. It was in the vicinity of a chain of lakes, and on the bank of the loveliest little stream, called the Bark river, which flowed in rapid amber brightness, through fields, and dells, and stately knolls, of most idylic beauty.

The little log cabin where we slept, with its flower garden in front, disturbed the scene no more than a stray lock on the fair cheek. The hospitality of that house I may well call princely; it was the boundless hospitality of the heart, which, if it has no Aladdin's lamp to create a palace for the guest, does him still higher service by the freedom of its bounty up to the very last drop of its powers.

Sweet were the sunsets seen in the valley of this stream, though here, and, I grieve to say, no less near the Rock River, the fiend, who has ever liberty to tempt the happy in this world, appeared in the shape of mosquitoes, and allowed us no bodily to enjoy our mental peace.

One day we ladies gave, under the guidance of our host, to visiting all the beauties of the adjacent lakes--Nomabbin, Silver, and Pine Lakes. On the shore of Nomabbin had formerly been one of the finest Indian villages. Our host said that, one day, as he was lying there beneath the bank, he saw a tall Indian standing at gaze on the knoll. He lay a long time, curious to see how long the figure would maintain its statue-like absorption. But, at last, his patience yielded, and, in moving, he made a slight noise. The Indian saw him, gave a wild, snorting sound of indignation and pain, and strode away.

What feelings must consume their heart at such moments! I scarcely see how they can forbear to shoot the white man where he stands.

But the power of fate is with the white man, and the Indian feels it. This same gentleman told of his travelling through the wilderness with an Indian guide. He had with him a bottle of spirit which he meant to give him in small quantities, but the Indian, once excited, wanted the whole at once. I would not, said Mr.----, give it him, for I thought if he got really drunk, there was an end to his services as a guide. But he persisted, and at last tried to take it from me. I was not armed; he was, and twice as strong as I. But I knew an Indian could not resist the look of a white man, and I fixed my eye steadily on his. He bore it for a moment, then his eye fell; he let go the bottle. I took his gun and threw it to a distance. After a few moments' pause, I told him to go and fetch it, and left it in his hands. From that moment he was quite obedient, even servile, all the rest of the way.

This gentleman, though in other respects of most kindly and liberal heart, showed the aversion that the white man soon learns to feel for the Indian on whom he encroaches, the aversion of the injurer for him he has degraded. After telling the anecdote of his seeing the Indian gazing at the seat of his former home,

"A thing for human feelings the most trying,"

and which, one would think, would have awakened soft compassion--almost remorse--in the present owner of that fair hill, which contained for the exile the bones of his dead, the ashes of his hopes,--he observed, "They cannot be prevented from straggling back here to their old haunts. I wish they could. They ought not to permitted to drive away *our* game." OUR game--just heavens!

The same gentleman showed, on a slight occasion, the true spirit of the sportsman, or, perhaps I might say of Man, when engaged in any kind of chase. Showing us some antlers, he said, "This one belonged to a majestic creature. But this other was the beauty. I had been lying a long time at watch, when at last I heard them come crackling along. I lifted my head cautiously, as they burst through the trees. The first was a magnificent fellow; but then I saw coming one, the prettiest, the most graceful I ever beheld--there was something so soft and beseeching in its look. I chose him at once; took aim, and shot him dead. You see the antlers are not very large; it was young, but the prettiest creature!"

In the course of this morning's drive, we visited the gentlemen on their fishing party. They hailed us gaily, and rowed ashore to show us what fine booty they had.

No disappointment there, no dull work. On the beautiful point of land from which we first saw them, lived a contented woman, the only one I heard of out there. She was English, and said she had seen so much suffering in her own country that the hardships of this seemed as nothing to her. But the others--even our sweet and gentle hostess--found their labors disproportioned to their strength, if not to their patience; and, while their husbands and brothers enjoyed the country in hunting or fishing, they found themselves confined to a comfortless and laborious indoor life. But it need not be so long.

This afternoon, driving about on the banks of these lakes, we found the scene all of one kind of loveliness; wide, graceful woods, and then these fine sheets of water, with fine points of land jutting out boldly into them. It was lovely, but not striking or peculiar.

All woods suggest pictures. The European forest, with its long glades and green sunny dells, naturally suggested the figures of armed knight on his proud steed, or maiden, decked in gold and pearl, pricking along them on a snow white palfrey. The green dells, of weary Palmer sleeping there beside the spring with his head upon his wallet. Our minds, familiar with such figures, people with them the New England woods, wherever the sunlight falls down a longer than usual cart-track, wherever a cleared spot has lain still enough for the trees to look friendly, with their exposed sides cultivated by the light, and the grass to look velvet warm, and be embroidered with flowers. These western woods suggest a different kind of ballad. The Indian legends have, often, an air of the wildest solitude, as has the one Mr. Lowell has put into verse, in his late volume. But I did not see those wild woods; only such as suggest little romances of love and sorrow, like this:

> A maiden sat beneath the tree,
> Tear-bedewed her pale cheeks be,
> And she sigheth heavily.
>
> From forth the wood into the light,
> A hunter strides with carol light,
> And a glance so bold and bright.

He careless stopped and eyed the maid;
"Why weepest thou?" he gently said,
"I love thee well; be not afraid."

He takes her hand, and leads her on;
She should have waited there alone,
For he was not her chosen one.

He leans her head upon his breast,
She knew 't was not her home of rest,
But ah! she had been sore distrest.

The sacred stars looked sadly down;
The parting moon appeared to frown,
To see thus dimmed the diamond crown.

Then from the thicket starts a deer,
The huntsman, seizing on his spear,
Cries, "Maiden, wait thou for me here."

She sees him vanish into night,
She starts from sleep in deep affright,
For it was not her own true knight.

Though but in dream Gunhilda failed;
Though but a fancied ill assailed,
Though she but fancied fault bewailed.

Yet thought of day makes dream of night:
She is not worthy of the knight,
The inmost altar burns not bright.

If loneliness thou canst not bear,
Cannot the dragon's venom dare,
Of the pure meed thou shouldst despair.

Now sadder that lone maiden sighs,
Far bitterer tears profane her eyes,
Crushed in the dust her heart's flower lies.

On the bank of Silver Lake we saw an Indian encampment. A shower threatened us, but we resolved to try if we could not visit it before it came on. We crossed a wide field on foot, and found them amid the trees on a shelving bank; just as we reached them the rain began to fall in torrents, with frequent thunder claps, and we had to take refuge in their lodges. These were very small, being for temporary use, and we crowded the occupants much, among whom were several sick, on the damp ground, or with only a ragged mat between them and it. But they showed all the gentle courtesy which marks them towards the stranger, who stands in any need; though it was obvious that the visit, which inconvenienced them, could only have been caused by the most impertinent curiosity, they made us as comfortable as their extreme poverty permitted. They seemed to think we would not like to touch them: a sick girl in the lodge where I was, persisted in moving so as to give me the dry place; a woman with the sweet melancholy eye of the race, kept off the children and wet dogs from even the hem of my garment.

Without, their fires smouldered, and black kettles, hung over them on sticks, smoked and seethed in the rain. An old theatrical looking Indian stood with arms folded, looking up to the heavens, from which the rain dashed and the thunder reverberated; his air was French-Roman, that is, more romanesque than Roman. The Indian ponies, much excited, kept careering through the wood, around the encampment, and now and then halting suddenly, would thrust in their intelligent, though amazed, phizzes, as if to ask their masters when this awful pother would cease, and then, after a moment, rush and trample off again.

At last we got off, well wetted, but with a picturesque scene for memory. At a house where we stopped to get dry, they told us that this wandering band (of Pottawattamies,) who had returned on a visit, either from homesickness, or need of relief, were extremely destitute. The women had been there to see if they could barter their head bands with which they club their hair behind into a form not unlike a Grecian knot, for food. They seemed, indeed, to have neither food, utensils, clothes, nor bedding; nothing but the ground, the sky, and their own strength. Little wonder if they drove off the game!

Part of the same band I had seen in Milwaukie, on a begging dance. The effect of this was wild and grotesque. They wore much paint and feather head-dresses. "Indians without paint are poor coots," said a gentleman who had been a great deal with, and really liked, them; and I like the effect of the paint on them; it reminds of the gay fantasies of nature. With them in Milwaukie, was a chief, the finest Indian figure I saw, more than six feet in height, erect, and of a sullen, but grand gait and gesture. He wore a deep red blanket, which fell in large folds from his shoulders to his feet, did not join in the dance, but slowly strode about through the streets, a fine sight, not a French-Roman, but a real Roman. He looked unhappy, but listlessly unhappy, as if he felt it was of no use to strive or resist.

While in the neighborhood of these lakes, we visited also a foreign settlement of great interest. Here were minds, it seemed, to "comprehend the trusts," of their new life; and if they can only stand true to them, will derive and bestow great benefits therefrom.

But sad and sickening to the enthusiast who comes to these shores, hoping the tranquil enjoyment of intellectual blessings, and the pure happiness of mutual love, must be a part of the scene that he encounters at first. He has escaped from the heartlessness of courts, to encounter the vulgarity of a mob; he has secured solitude, but it is a lonely, a deserted solitude. Amid the abundance of nature he cannot, from petty, but insuperable obstacles, procure, for a long time, comforts, or a home.

But let him come sufficiently armed with patience to learn the new spells which the new dragons require, (and this can only be done on the spot,) he will not finally be disappointed of the promised treasure; the mob will resolve itself into men, yet crude, but of good dispositions, and capable of good character; the solitude will become sufficiently enlivened and home grow up at last from the rich sod.

In this transition state we found one of these homes. As we approached it seemed the very Eden which earth might still afford to a pair willing to give up the hackneyed pleasures of the world, for a better and more intimate communion with one another and with beauty: the wild road led through wide beautiful woods, to the wilder and more beautiful shores of the finest lake we saw. On its waters, glittering in the morning sun, a few Indians were paddling to and fro in their light canoes. On one of those fair knolls I have so often mentioned, stood the cottage, beneath trees which stooped as if they yet felt brotherhood with its roof tree. Flowers waved, birds fluttered round, all had the sweetness of a happy seclusion; all invited on entrance to cry, All hail ye happy ones! to those who inhabited it.

But on entrance to those evidently rich in personal beauty, talents, love, and courage, the aspect of things was rather sad. Sickness had been with them, death, care, and labor; these had not yet blighted them, but had turned their gay smiles grave. It seemed that hope and joy had given place to resolution. How much, too, was there in them, worthless in this place, which would have been so valuable elsewhere. Refined graces, cultivated powers, shine in vain before field laborers, as laborers are in this present world; you might as well cultivate heliotropes to present to an ox. Oxen and heliotropes are both good, but not for one another.

With them were some of the old means of enjoyment, the books, the pencil, the guitar; but where the wash-tub and the axe are so constantly in requisition, there is not much time and pliancy of hand for these.

In the inner room the master of the house was seated; he had been sitting there long, for he had injured his foot on ship-board, and his farming had to be done by proxy. His beautiful young wife was his only attendant and nurse, as well as a farm housekeeper; how well she performed hard and unaccustomed duties, the objects of her care shewed; everything that belonged to the house was rude but neatly arranged; the invalid, confined to an uneasy wooden chair, (they had not been able to induce any one to bring them an easy chair from the town,) looked as neat and elegant as if he had been dressed by the valet of a duke. He was of northern blood, with clear full blue eyes, calm features, a tempering of the soldier, scholar, and man of the world, in his aspect; whether that various intercourses had given himself that thorough-bred look never seen in Americans, or that it was inherited from a race who had known all these disciplines. He formed a great but pleasing contrast to his wife, whose glowing complexion and dark mellow eye bespoke an origin in some climate more familiar with the sun. He looked as if he could sit there a great while patiently, and live on his own mind, biding his time; she, as if she could bear anything for affection's sake, but would feel the weight of each moment as it passed.

Seeing the album full of drawings and verses which bespoke the circle of elegant and affectionate intercourse they had left, behind, we could not but see that the young wife sometimes must need a sister, the husband a companion, and both must often miss that electricity which sparkles from the chain of congenial minds.

For man, a position is desirable in some degree proportioned to his education. Mr. Birkbeck was bred a farmer, but these were nurslings of the court and city; they may persevere, for an affectionate courage shone in their eyes, and, if so, become true lords of the soil, and informing geniuses to those around; then, perhaps, they will feel that they have not paid too dear for the tormented independence of the new settler's life. But, generally, damask roses will not thrive in the wood, and a ruder growth, if healthy and pure, we wish rather to see there.

I feel very differently about these foreigners from Americans; American men and women are inexcusable if they do not bring up children so as to be fit for vicissitudes; that is the meaning of our star, that here all men being free and equal, all should be fitted for freedom and an independence by his own resources wherever the changeful wave of our mighty stream may take him. But the star of Europe brought a different horoscope, and to mix destinies breaks the thread of both. The Arabian horse will not plough well, nor can the plough-horse be rode to play the jereed. But a man is a man wherever he goes, and something precious cannot fail to be gained by one who knows how to abide by a resolution of any kind, and pay the cost without a murmur.

Returning, the fine carriage at last fulfilled its threat of breaking down. We took refuge in a farm house. Here was a pleasant scene. A rich and beautiful estate, several happy families, who had removed together, and formed a natural community, ready to help and enliven one another. They were farmers at home, in western New York, and both men and women knew how to work. Yet even here the women did not like the change, but they were willing, "as it might be best for the young folks." Their hospitality was great, the housefull of women and pretty children seemed all of one mind.

Returning to Milwaukie much fatigued, I entertained myself for a day or two with reading. The book I had brought with me was in strong contrast with the life around me. Very strange was this vision of an exalted and sensitive existence, which seemed to invade the next sphere, in contrast with the spontaneous, instinctive life, so healthy and so near the ground I had been surveying. This was the German book entitled:

Die Scherin von Prevorst.--Eroeffnungen ueber das innere Leben des Menschen und ueber das hereinragen einer Geisterwelt in die unsere. Mitgetheilt von Justinus Kerner.

The Seeress of Prevorst.--Revelations concerning the inward life of man, and the projection of a world of spirits into ours, communicated by Justinus Kerner.

This book, published in Germany some twelve years since, and which called forth there plenteous dews of admiration, as plenteous hail-storms of jeers and scorns, I never saw mentioned till some year or two since, in any English publication. Then a playful, but not sarcastic account of it, in the Dublin Magazine, so far excited my curiosity that I procured the book intending to read it so soon as I should have some leisure days, such as this journey has afforded.

Dr. Kerner, its author, is a man of distinction in his native land, both as a physician and a thinker, though always on the side of reverence, marvel, and mysticism. He was known to me only through two or three little poems of his in Catholic legends, which I much admired for the fine sense they showed of the beauty of symbols.

He here gives a biography, mental and physical, of one of the most remarkable cases of high nervous excitement that the age, so interested in such, yet affords, with all its phenomena of clairvoyance and susceptibility of magnetic influences. I insert some account of this biography at the request of many who have been interested by slight references to it. The book, a thick and heavy volume, written with true German patience, some would say clumsiness, has not, probably, and may not be translated into other languages. As to my own mental position on these subjects it may be briefly expressed by a dialogue between several persons who honor me with a portion of friendly confidence and of criticism, and myself expressed as *Free Hope*. The others may be styled *Old Church, Good Sense*, and *Self-Poise*.

Good Sense. I wonder you can take any interest in such observations or experiments. Don't you see how almost impossible it is to make them with any exactness, how entirely impossible to know anything about them unless made by yourself, when the least leaven of credulity, excited fancy, to say nothing of willing or careless imposture, spoils the whole loaf. Beside, allowing the possibility of some clear glimpses into a higher state of being, what do we want of it now? All around us lies what we neither understand nor use. Our capacities, our instincts for this our present sphere are but half developed. Let us confine ourselves to that till the lesson be learned; let us be completely natural, before we trouble ourselves with the supernatural. I never see any of these things but I long to get away and lie under a green tree and let the wind blow on me. There is marvel and charm enough in that for me.

Free Hope. And for me also. Nothing is truer than the Wordsworthian creed, on which Carlyle lays such stress, that we need only look on the miracle of every day, to sate ourselves with thought and admiration every day. But how are our faculties sharpened to do it? Precisely by apprehending the infinite results of every day.

Who sees the meaning of the flower uprooted in the ploughed field? The ploughman who does not look beyond its boundaries and does not raise his eyes from the ground? No--but the poet who sees that field in its relations with the universe, and looks oftener to the sky than on the ground. Only the dreamer shall understand realities, though, in truth, his dreaming must not be out of proportion to his waking!

The mind, roused powerfully by this existence, stretches of itself into what the French sage calls the "aromal state." From the hope thus gleaned it forms the hypothesis, under whose banner it collects its facts.

Long before these slight attempts were made to establish as a science what is at present called animal magnetism, always, in fact men were occupied more or less with this vital principle, principle of flux and influx, dynamic of our mental mechanics, human phase of electricity. Poetic observation was pure, there was no quackery in its free course, as there is so often in this wilful tampering with the hidden springs of life, for it is tampering unless done in a patient spirit and with severe truth; yet it may be, by the rude or greedy miners, some good ore is unearthed. And some there are who work in the true temper, patient and accurate in trial, not rushing to conclusions, feeling there is a mystery, not eager to call it by name, till they can know it as a reality: such may learn, such may teach.

Subject to the sudden revelations, the breaks in habitual existence caused by the aspect of death, the touch of love, the flood of music, I never lived, that I remember, what you call a common natural day. All my days are touched by the supernatural, for I feel the pressure of hidden causes, and the presence, sometimes the communion, of unseen powers. It needs not that I should ask the clairvoyant whether "a spirit-world projects into ours." As to the specific evidence, I would not tarnish my mind by hasty reception. The mind is not, I know, a highway, but a temple, and its doors should not be carelessly left open. Yet it were sin, if indolence or coldness excluded what had a claim to enter; and I doubt whether, in the eyes of pure intelligence, an ill-grounded hasty rejection be not a greater sign of weakness than an ill-grounded and hasty faith.

I will quote, as my best plea, the saying of a man old in years, but not in heart, and whose long life has been distinguished by that clear adaptation of means to ends which gives the credit of practical wisdom. He wrote to his child, "I have lived too long, and seen too much to be incredulous." Noble the thought, no less so its frank expression, instead of saws of caution, mean advices, and other modern instances. Such was the romance of Socrates when he bade his disciples "sacrifice a cock to Aesculapius."

Old Church. You are always so quick-witted and voluble, Free Hope, you don't get time to see how often you err, and even, perhaps, sin and blaspheme. The Author of all has intended to confine our knowledge within certain boundaries, has given us a short span of time for a certain probation, for which our faculties are adapted. By wild speculation and intemperate curiosity we violate his will and incur dangerous, perhaps fatal, consequences. We waste our powers, and, becoming morbid and visionary, are unfitted to obey positive precepts, and perform positive duties.

Free Hope. I do not see how it is possible to go further beyond the results of a limited human experience than those do who pretend to settle the origin and nature of sin, the final destiny of souls, and the whole plan of the causal spirit with regard to them. I think those who take your view, have not examined themselves, and do not know the ground on which they stand.

I acknowledge no limit, set up by man's opinion, as to the capacities of man. "Care is taken," I see it, "that the trees grow not up into heaven," but, to me it seems, the more vigorously they aspire the better. Only let it be a vigorous, not a partial or sickly aspiration. Let not the tree forget its root.

So long as the child insists on knowing where its dead parent is, so long as bright eyes weep at mysterious pressures, too heavy for the life, so long as that impulse is constantly arising which made the Roman emperor address his soul in a strain of such touching softness, vanishing from the thought, as the column of smoke from the eye, I know of no inquiry which the impulse of man suggests that is forbidden to the resolution of man to pursue. In every inquiry, unless sustained by a pure and reverent spirit, he gropes in the dark, or falls headlong.

Self-Poise. All this may be very true, but what is the use of all this straining? Far-sought is dear-bought. When we know that all is in each, and that the ordinary contains the extraordinary, why should we play the baby, and insist upon having the moon for a toy when a tin dish will do as well. Our deep ignorance is a chasm that we can only fill up by degrees, but the commonest rubbish will help us as well as shred silk. The God Brahma, while on earth, was set to fill up a valley, but he had only a basket given him in which to fetch earth for this purpose; so is it with us all. No leaps, no starts will avail us, by patient crystallization alone the equal temper of wisdom is attainable. Sit at home and the spirit-world will look in at your window with moonlit eyes; run out to find it, and rainbow and golden cup will have vanished and left you the beggarly child you were. The better part of wisdom is a sublime prudence, a pure and patient truth that will receive nothing it is not sure it can permanently lay to heart. Of our study there should be in proportion two-thirds of rejection to one of acceptance. And, amid the manifold infatuations and illusions of this world of emotion, a being capable of clear intelligence can do no better service than to hold himself upright, avoid nonsense, and do what chores lie in his way, acknowledging every moment that primal truth, which no fact exhibits, nor, if pressed by too warm a hope, will even indicate. I think, indeed, it is part of our lesson to give a formal consent to what is farcical, and to pick up our living and our virtue amid what is so ridiculous, hardly deigning a smile, and certainly not vexed. The work is done through all, if not by every one.

Free Hope. Thou art greatly wise, my friend, and ever respected by me, yet I find not in your theory or your scope, room enough for the lyric inspirations, or the mysterious whispers of life. To me it seems that it is madder never to abandon oneself, than often to be infatuated; better to be wounded, a captive, and a slave, than always to walk in armor. As to magnetism, that is only a matter of fancy. You sometimes need just such a field in which to wander vagrant, and if it bear a higher name, yet it may be that, in last result, the trance of Pythagoras might be classed with the more infantine transports of the Seeress of Prevorst.

What is done interests me more than what is thought and supposed. Every fact is impure, but every fact contains in it the juices of life. Every fact is a clod, from which may grow an amaranth or a palm.

Do you climb the snowy peaks from whence come the streams, where the atmosphere is rare, where you can see the sky nearer, from which you can get a commanding view of the landscape. I see great disadvantages as well as advantages in this dignified position. I had rather walk myself through all kinds of places, even at the risk of being robbed in the forest, half drowned at the ford, and covered with dust in the street.

I would beat with the living heart of the world, and understand all the moods, even the fancies or fantasies, of nature. I dare to trust to the interpreting spirit to bring me out all right at last--to establish truth through error.

Whether this be the best way is of no consequence, if it be the one individual character points out.

> For one, like me, it would be vain
> From glittering heights the eyes to strain;
> I the truth can only know,
> Tested by life's most fiery glow.
> Seeds of thought will never thrive
> Till dews of love shall bid them live.

Let me stand in my age with all its waters flowing round me. If they sometimes subdue, they must finally upbear me, for I seek the Universal--and that must be the best.

The Spirit, no doubt, leads in every movement of my time: if I seek the How, I shall find it, as well as if I busied myself more with the Why.

Whatever is, is right, if only men are steadily bent to make it so, by comprehending and fulfilling its design.

May not I have an office, too, in my hospitality and ready sympathy? If I sometimes entertain guests who cannot pay with gold coin, with "fair rose nobles," that is better than to lose the chance of entertaining angels unawares.

You, my three friends, are held in heart-honor, by me. You, especially, Good-Sense, because where you do not go yourself, you do not object to another's going, if he will. You are really liberal. You, Old Church, are of use, by keeping unforgot the effigies of old religion, and reviving the tone of pure Spenserian sentiment, which this time is apt to stifle in its childish haste. But you are very faulty in censuring and wishing to limit others by your own standard. You, Self-Poise, fill a priestly office. Could but a larger intelligence of the vocations of others, and a tender sympathy with their individual natures be added, had you more of love, or more of apprehensive genius, (for either would give you the needed expansion and delicacy) you would command my entire reverence. As it is, I must at times deny and oppose you, and so must others, for you tend, by your influence, to exclude us from our full, free life. We must be content when you censure, and rejoiced when you approve; always admonished to good by your whole being, and sometimes by your judgment. And so I pass on to interest myself and others in the memoir of the Scherin von Prevorst.

Aside from Loewenstein, a town of Wirtemberg, on mountains whose highest summit is more than eighteen hundred feet above the level of the sea, lies in romantic seclusion, surrounded on all sides by woods and hills, the hamlet of Prevorst.

Its inhabitants number about four hundred and fifty, most of whom support themselves by wood-cutting, and making charcoal, and collecting wood seed.

As is usual with those who live upon the mountains, these are a vigorous race, and generally live to old age without sickness. Diseases that infest the valley, such as ague, never touch them; but they are subject in youth to attacks upon the nerves, which one would not expect in so healthy a class. In a town situated near to, and like Prevorst, the children were often attacked with a kind of St. Vitus's dance. They would foresee when it would seize upon them, and, if in the field, would hasten home to undergo the paroxysms there. From these they rose, as from magnetic sleep, without memory of what had happened.

Other symptoms show the inhabitants of this region very susceptible to magnetic and sidereal influences.

On this mountain, and indeed in the hamlet of Prevorst, was, in 1801, a woman born, in whom a peculiar inner life discovered itself from early childhood. Frederica Hauffe, whose father was gamekeeper of this district of forest, was, as the position and solitude of her birthplace made natural, brought up in the most simple manner. In the keen mountain air and long winter cold, she was not softened by tenderness either as to dress or bedding, but grew up lively and blooming; and while her brothers and sisters, under the same circumstances, were subject to rheumatic attacks, she remained free from them. On the other hand, her peculiar tendency displayed itself in her dreams. If anything affected her painfully, if her mind was excited by reproof, she had instructive warning, or prophetic dreams.

While yet quite young, her parents let her go, for the advantages of instruction, to her grandfather, Johann Schmidgall, in Loewenstein.

Here were discovered in her the sensibility to magnetic and ghostly influences, which, the good Kerner assures us, her grandparents deeply lamented, and did all in their power to repress. But, as it appears that her grandfather, also, had seen a ghost, and there were evidently legends in existence about the rooms in which the little Frederika saw ghosts, and spots where the presence of human bones caused her sudden shivering, we may be allowed to doubt whether indirect influence was not more powerful than direct repression upon these subjects.

There is the true German impartiality with regard to the scene of appearance for these imposing visiters; sometimes it is "a room in the Castle of Loewenstein, long disused," a la Radcliffe, sometimes "a deserted kitchen."

This "solemn, unhappy gift," brought no disturbance to the childish life of the maiden, she enjoyed life with more vivacity than most of her companions. The only trouble she had was the extreme irritability of the optic nerve, which, though without inflammation of the eyes, sometimes confined her to a solitary chamber. "This," says Dr. K. "was probably a sign of the development of the spiritual in the fleshly eye."

Sickness of her parents at last called her back to the lonely Prevorst, where, by trouble and watching beside sick beds, her feelings were too much excited, so that the faculty for prophetic dreams and the vision of spirits increased upon her.

From her seventeenth to her nineteenth year, when every outward relation was pleasant for her, this inward life was not so active, and she was distinguished from other girls of her circle only by the more intellectual nature, which displayed itself chiefly in the eyes, and by a greater liveliness which, however, never passed the bounds of grace and propriety.

She had none of the sentimentality so common at that age, and it can be proved that she had never an attachment, nor was disappointed in love, as has been groundlessly asserted.

In her nineteenth year, she was by her family betrothed to Herr H. The match was desirable on account of the excellence of the man, and the sure provision it afforded for her comfort through life.

But, whether from presentiment of the years of suffering that were before her, or from other hidden feelings, of which we only know with certainty that, if such there were, they were not occasioned by another attachment, she sank into a dejection, inexplicable to her family; passed whole days in weeping; scarcely slept for some weeks, and thus the life of feeling which had been too powerful in her childhood was called up anew in full force.

On the day of her solemn betrothal, took place, also, the funeral of T., the preacher of Oberstenfeld, a man of sixty and more years, whose preaching, instruction, and character, (he was goodness itself,) had had great influence upon her life. She followed the dear remains, with others, to the church-yard. Her heart till then so heavy, was suddenly relieved and calmed, as she stood beside the grave. She remained there long, enjoying her new peace, and when she went away found herself tranquil, but indifferent to all the concerns of this world. Here began the period, not indeed as yet of sickness, but of her peculiar inward life, which knew afterward no pause.

Later, in somnambulic state, she spoke of this day in the following verses. The deceased had often appeared to her as a shape of light, protecting her from evil spirits.

(These are little simple rhymes; they are not worth translating into verse, though, in the original, they have a childish grace.)

>
> What was once so dark to me,
> I see now clearly.
> In that day
> When I had given in marriage myself away,

> I stood quite immersed in thee,
> Thou angel figure above thy grave mound.
> Willingly would I have exchanged with thee,
> Willingly given up to thee my earthly luck,
> Which those around praised as the blessing of heaven.
>
>   I prayed upon thy grave
>   For one blessing only,
>   That the wings of this angel
>   Might henceforward
>   On the hot path of life,
>   Waft around me the peace of heaven.
> There standest thou, angel, now; my prayer was heard.

She was, in consequence of her marriage, removed to Kuernbach, a place on the borders of Wuertemberg and Baden. Its position is low, gloomy, shut in by hills; opposite in all the influences of earth and atmosphere to those of Prevorst and its vicinity.

Those of electrical susceptibility are often made sick or well by change of place. Papponi, (of whom Amoretti writes,) a man of such susceptibility, was cured of convulsive attacks by change of place. Penriet could find repose while in one part of Calabria, only by wrapping himself in an oil-cloth mantle, thus, as it were, isolating himself. That great sense of sidereal and imponderable influences, which afterward manifested itself so clearly in the Seherin, probably made this change of place very unfavorable to her. Later, it appeared, that the lower she came down from the hills, the more she suffered from spasms, but on the heights her tendency to the magnetic state was the greatest.

But also mental influences were hostile to her. Already withdrawn from the outward life, she was placed, where, as consort and housekeeper to a laboring man, the calls on her care and attention were incessant. She was obliged hourly to forsake her inner home, to provide for an outer, which did not correspond with it.

She bore this seven months, though flying to solitude, whenever outward relations permitted. But longer it was not possible to conceal the inward verity by an outward action, "the body sank beneath the attempt, and the spirit took refuge in the inner circle."

One night she dreamed that she awoke and found the dead body of the preacher T. by her side; that at the same time her father, and two physicians were considering what should be done for her in a severe sickness. She called out that "the dead friend would help her; she needed no physician." Her husband, hearing her cry out in sleep, woke her.

This dream was presage of a fever, which seized her next morning. It lasted fourteen days with great violence, and was succeeded by attacks of convulsion and spasm. This was the beginning of that state of bodily suffering and mental exaltation in which she passed the remaining seven years of her life.

She seems to have been very injudiciously treated in the first stages of her illness. Bleeding was resorted to, as usual in cases of extreme suffering where the nurses know not what else to do, and, as usual, the momentary relief was paid for by an increased nervousness, and capacity for suffering.

Magnetic influences from other persons were of frequent use to her, but they were applied without care as to what characters and constitutions were brought into connexion with hers, and were probably in the end just as injurious to her as the loss of blood. At last she became so weak, so devoid of all power in herself, that her life seemed entirely dependent on artificial means and the influence of other men.

There is a singular story of a woman in the neighborhood, who visited her once or twice, apparently from an instinct that she should injure her, and afterwards, interfered in the same way, and with the same results, in the treatment of her child.

This demoniacal impulse and power, which were ascribed to the Canidias of ancient superstition, may be seen subtly influencing the members of every-day society. We see persons led, by an uneasy impulse, towards the persons and the topics where they are sure they can irritate and annoy. This is constantly observable among children, also in the closest relations between grown up people who have not yet the government of themselves, neither are governed by the better power.

There is also an interesting story of a quack who treated her with amulets, whose parallel may be found in the action of such persons in common society. It is an expression of the power that a vulgar and self-willed nature will attain over one delicate, poetical, but not yet clear within itself; outwardly it yields to a power which it inwardly disclaims.

A touching little passage is related of a time in the first years, when she seemed to be better, so much so as to receive an evening visit from some female friends. They grew merry and began to dance; she remained sad and thoughtful. When they stopped, she was in the attitude of prayer. One of her intimates, observing this, began to laugh. This affected her so much, that she became cold and rigid like a corpse. For some time they did not hear her breathe, and, when she did, it was with a rattling noise. They applied mustard poultices, and used foot and hand baths; she was brought back to life, but to a state of great suffering.

She recognized as her guardian spirit, who sometimes magnetized her or removed from her neighborhood substances that were hurtful to her, her grandmother; thus coinciding with the popular opinion that traits reappear in the third generation.

Now began still greater wonders; the second sight, numerous and various visits from spirits and so forth.

The following may be mentioned in connection with theories and experiments current among ourselves.

"A friend, who was often with her at this time, wrote to me (Kerner): When I, with my finger, touch her **on the forehead between the eyebrows**, she says each time something that bears upon the state of my soul. Some of these sentences I record.

"Keep thy soul so that thou mayst bear it in thy hands."

"When thou comest into a world of bustle and folly, hold the Lord fast in thy heart."

"If any seek to veil from thee thy true feeling, pray to God for grace."

"Permit not thyself to stifle the light that springs up within thyself."

"Think often of the cross of Jesus; go forth and embrace it."

"As the dove found a resting-place in Noah's ark, so wilt thou, also, find a resting-place which God has appointed for thee."

When she was put under the care of Kerner, she had been five years in this state, and was reduced to such weakness, that she was, with difficulty, sustained from hour to hour.

He thought at first it would be best to take no notice of her magnetic states and directions, and told her he should not, but should treat her with regard to her bodily symptoms, as he would any other invalid.

"At this time she fell every evening into magnetic sleep, and gave orders about herself; to which, however, those round her no longer paid attention.

I was now called in. I had never seen this woman, but had heard many false or perverted accounts of her condition. I must confess that I shared the evil opinion of the world as to her illness; that I advised to pay no attention to her magnetic situation, and the orders she gave in it; in her spasms, to forbear the laying of hands upon her; to deny her the support of persons of stronger nerves; in short, to do all possible to draw her out of the magnetic state, and to treat her with attention, but with absolutely none but the common medical means.

These views were shared by my friend, Dr. Off, of Loewenstein, who continued to treat her accordingly. But without good results. Hemorrhage, spasms, night-sweats continued. Her gums were scorbutically affected, and bled constantly; she lost all her teeth. Strengthening remedies affected her like being drawn up from her bed by force; she sank into a fear of all men, and a deadly weakness. Her death was to be wished, but it came not. Her relations, in despair, not knowing themselves what they could do with her, brought her, almost against my will, to me at Weinsburg.

She was brought hither an image of death, perfectly emaciated, unable to raise herself. Every three or four minutes, a teaspoonful of nourishment must be given her, else she fell into faintness or convulsion. Her somnambulic situation alternated with fever, hemorrhage, and night-sweats. Every evening, about seven o'clock, she fell into magnetic sleep. She then spread out her arms, and found herself, from that moment, in a clairvoyant state; but only when she brought them back upon her breast, did she begin to speak. (Kerner mentions that her child, too, slept with its hands and feet crossed.) In this state her eyes were shut, her face calm and bright. As she fell asleep, the first night after her arrival, she asked for me, but I bade them tell her that I now, and in future, should speak to her only when awake.

After she awoke, I went to her and declared, in brief and earnest terms, that I should pay no attention to what she said in sleep, and that her somnambulic state, which had lasted so long to the grief and trouble of her family, must now come to an end. This declaration I accompanied by an earnest appeal, designed to awaken a firm will in her to put down the excessive activity of brain that disordered her whole system. Afterwards, no address was made to her on any subject when in her sleep-waking state. She was left to lie unheeded. I pursued a homoeopathic treatment of her case. But the medicines constantly produced effects opposite to what I expected. She now suffered less from spasm and somnambulism, but with increasing marks of weakness and decay. All seemed as if the end of her sufferings drew near. It was too late for the means I wished to use. Affected so variously and powerfully by magnetic means in the first years of her illness, she had now no life more, so thoroughly was the force of her own organization exhausted, but what she borrowed from others. In her now more infrequent magnetic trance, she was always seeking the true means of her cure. It was touching to see how, retiring within herself, she sought for help. The physician who had aided her so little with his drugs, must often stand abashed before this inner physician, perceiving it to be far better skilled than himself."

After some weeks forbearance, Kerner did ask her in her sleep what he should do for her. She prescribed a magnetic treatment, which was found of use. Afterwards, she described a machine, of which there is a drawing in this book, which she wished to have made for her use; it was so, and she derived benefit from it. She had indicated such a machine in the early stages of her disease, but at that time no one attended to her. By degrees she grew better under this treatment, and lived at Weinsberg, nearly two years, though in a state of great weakness, and more in the magnetic and clairvoyant than in the natural human state.

How his acquaintance with her affected the physician, he thus expresses:

"During those last months of her abode on the earth, there remained to her only the life of a sylph. I have been interested to record, not a journal of her sickness, but the mental phenomena of such an almost disembodied life. Such may cast light on the period when also our Psyche may unfold her wings, free from bodily bonds, and the hindrances of space and time. I give facts; each reader may interpret them in his own way.

The manuals of animal magnetism and other writings have proposed many theories by which to explain such. All these are known to me. I shall make no reference to them, but only, by use of parallel facts here and there, show that the phenomena of this case recall many in which there is nothing marvellous, but which are manifestly grounded in our common existence. Such apparitions cannot too frequently, if only for moments, flash across that common existence, as electric lights from the higher world.

Frau H. was, previous to my magnetic treatment, in so deep a somnambulic life, that she was, in fact, never rightly awake, even when she seemed to be; or rather, let us say, she was at all times more awake than others are; for it is strange to term sleep this state which is just that of the clearest wakefulness. Better to say she was immersed in the inward state.

In this state and the consequent excitement of the nerves, she had almost wholly lost organic force, and received it only by transmission from those of stronger condition, principally from their eyes and the ends of the fingers. The atmosphere and nerve communications of others, said she, bring me the life which I need; they do not feel it; these effusions on which I live, would flow from them and be lost, if my nerves did not attract them; only in this way can I live.

She often assured us that others did not suffer by loss of what they imparted to her; but it cannot be denied that persons were weakened by constant intercourse with her, suffered from contraction in the limbs, trembling, &c. They were weakened also in the eyes and pit of the stomach. From those related to her by blood, she could draw more benefit than from others, and, when very weak, from them only; probably on account of a natural affinity of temperament. She could not bear to have around her nervous and sick persons; those from whom she could gain nothing made her weaker.

Even so it is remarked that flowers soon lose their beauty near the sick, and suffer peculiarly under the contact or care of some persons.

Other physicians, beside myself, can vouch that the presence of some persons affected her as a pabulum vitae, while, if left with certain others or alone, she was sure to grow weaker.

From the air, too, she seemed to draw a peculiar ethereal nourishment of the same sort; she could not remain without an open window in the severest cold of winter.[1]

---

1 Near us, this last winter, a person who suffered, an finally died, from spasms like those of the Seherin, also found relief from having the windows open, while

The spirit of things, about which we have no perception, was sensible to her, and had influence on her; she showed this sense of the spirit of metals, plants, animals, and men. Imponderable existences, such as the various colors of the ray, showed distinct influences upon her. The electric fluid was visible and sensible to her when it was not to us. Yea! what is incredible! even the written words of men she could discriminate by touch.[2]

These experiments are detailed under their several heads in the book.

From her eyes flowed a peculiar spiritual light which impressed even those who saw her for a very short time. She was in each relation more spirit than human.

Should we compare her with anything human, we would say she was as one detained at the moment of dissolution, betwixt life and death; and who is better able to discern the affairs of the world that lies before, than that behind him.

She was often in situations when one who had, like her, the power of discerning spirits, would have seen her own free from the body, which at all times enveloped it only as a light veil. She saw herself often out of the body; saw herself double. She would say, "I seem out of myself, hover above my body, and think of it as something apart from myself. But it is not a pleasant feeling, because I still sympathize with my body. If only my soul were bound more firmly to the nerve-spirit, it might be bound more closely with the nerves themselves; but the bond of my nerve-spirit is always becoming looser."

She makes a distinction between spirit as the pure intelligence; soul, the ideal of this individual man; and nerve-spirit, the dynamic of his temporal existence.

Of this feeling of double identity, an invalid, now wasting under nervous disease, often speaks to me. He has it when he first awakes from sleep. Blake, the painter, whose life was almost as much a series of trances as that of our Seherin, in his designs of the Resurrection, represents spirits as rising from, or hovering over, their bodies in the same way.

Often she seemed quite freed from her body, and to have no more sense of its weight.

As to artificial culture, or dressing, (dressur,) Frau H. had nothing of it. She had learned no foreign tongue, neither history, nor geography, nor natural philosophy,

---

the cold occasioned great suffering to his attendants.
2 Facts of the same kind are asserted of late among ourselves, and believed, though "incredible."

nor any other of those branches now imparted to those of her sex in their schools. The Bible and hymn-book were, especially in the long years of her sickness, her only reading: her moral character was throughout blameless; she was pious without fanaticism. Even her long suffering, and the peculiar manner of it, she recognized as the grace of God; as she expresses in the following verses:

    Great God! how great is thy goodness,
      To me thou hast given faith and love,
  Holding me firm in the distress of my sufferings.

    In the darkness of my sorrow,
      I was so far led away,
  As to beg for peace in speedy death.

    But then came to me the mighty strong faith;
      Hope came; and came eternal love;
  They shut my earthly eyelids.
      When, O bliss!

    Dead lies my bodily frame,
      But in the inmost mind a light burns up,
  Such as none knows in the waking life.
      Is it a light? no! but a sun of grace!

Often in the sense of her sufferings, while in the magnetic trance, she made prayers in verse, of which this is one:

    Father, hear me!
    Hear my prayer and supplication.
      Father, I implore thee,
    Let not thy child perish!
      Look on my anguish, my tears.

> Shed hope into my heart, and still its longing,
> Father, on thee I call; have pity!
> Take something from me, the sick one, the poor one.

> Father, I leave thee not,
> Though sickness and pain consume me.
> If I the spring's light,
> See only through the mist of tears,
> Father, I leave thee not.

These verses lose their merit of a touching simplicity in an unrhymed translation; but they will serve to show the habitual temper of her mind.

"As I was a maker of verses," continues Dr. Kerner, "it was easy to say, Frau H. derived this talent from my magnetic influence; but she made these little verses before she came under my care." Not without deep significance was Apollo distinguished as being at once the God of poesy, of prophecy, and the medical art. Sleep-waking develops the powers of seeing, healing, and poesy. How nobly the ancients understood the inner life; how fully is it indicated in their mysteries?

I know a peasant maiden, who cannot write, but who, in the magnetic state, speaks in measured verse.

Galen was indebted to his nightly dreams for a part of his medical knowledge.

The calumnies spread about Frau H. were many and gross; this she well knew. As one day she heard so many of these as to be much affected by them, we thought she would express her feelings that night in the magnetic sleep, but she only said "they can affect my body, but not my spirit." Her mind, raised above such assaults by the consciousness of innocence, maintained its tranquillity and dwelt solely on spiritual matters.

Once in her sleep-waking she wrote thus:

> When the world declares of me
> Such cruel ill in calumny,
> And to your ears it finds a way,
> Do you believe it, yea or nay?

I answered:

> To us thou seemest true and pure,
>   Let others view it as they will;
>   We have our assurance still
> If our own sight can make us sure.

People of all kinds, to my great trouble, were always pressing to see her. If we refused them access to the sick room, they avenged themselves by the invention of all kinds of falsehoods.

She met all with an equal friendliness, even when it cost her bodily pain, and those who defamed her, she often defended. There came to her both good and bad men. She felt the evil in men clearly, but would not censure; lifted up a stone to cast at no sinner, but was rather likely to awake, in the faulty beings she suffered near her, faith in a spiritual life which might make them better.

Years before she was brought to me, the earth, with its atmosphere, and all that is about and upon it, human beings not excepted, was no more for her. She needed, not only a magnetizer, not only a love, an earnestness, an insight, such as scarce lies within the capacity of any man, but also what no mortal could bestow upon her, another heaven, other means of nourishment, other air than that of this earth. She belonged to the world of spirits, living here herself, as more than half spirit. She belonged to the state after death, into which she had advanced more than half way.

It is possible she might have been brought back to an adaptation for this world in the second or third year of her malady; but, in the fifth, no mode of treatment could have effected this. But by care she was aided to a greater harmony and clearness of the inward life; she enjoyed at Weinsberg, as she after said, the richest and happiest days of this life, and to us her abode here remains a point of light.

As to her outward form, we have already said it seemed but a thin veil about her spirit. She was little, her features of an oriental cast, her eye had the penetrating look of a seer's eye, which was set off by the shade of long dark eyelashes. She was a light flower that only lived on rays.

Eschenmayer writes thus of her in his "Mysteries."

"Her natural state was a mild, friendly earnestness, always disposed to prayer and devotion; her eye had a highly spiritual expression, and remained, notwithstanding her great sufferings, always bright and clear. Her look was penetrating, would quickly change in the conversation, seem to give forth sparks, and remain fixed on some one place,--this was a token that some strange apparition fettered it,--then would she resume the conversation. When I first saw her, she was in a situation which showed that her bodily life could not long endure, and that recovery to the common natural state was quite impossible. Without visible derangement of the functions, her life seemed only a wick glimmering in the socket. She was, as Kerner truly describes her, like one arrested in the act of dying and detained in the body by magnetic influences. Spirit and soul seemed often divided, and the spirit to have taken up its abode in other regions, while the soul was yet bound to the body."

I have given these extracts as being happily expressive of the relation between the physician and the clairvoyant, also of her character.

It seems to have been one of singular gentleness, and grateful piety, simple and pure, but not at all one from which we should expect extraordinary development of brain in any way; yet the excitement of her temperament from climate, scenery, the influence of traditions which evidently flowed round her, and a great constitutional impressibility did develop in her brain the germs both of poetic creation and science.

I say poetic creation, for, to my mind, the ghosts she saw were projections of herself into objective reality. The Hades she imagines is based in fact, for it is one of souls, who, having neglected their opportunities for better life, find themselves left forlorn, helpless, seeking aid from beings still ignorant and prejudiced, perhaps much below themselves in natural powers. Having forfeited their chance of direct access to God, they seek mediation from the prayers of men. But in the coloring and dress[3] of these ghosts, as also in their manner and mode of speech, there is a great deal which seems merely fanciful--local and peculiar.

To me, these interviews represent only prophecies of her mind; yet, considered in this way, they are, if not ghostly, spiritual facts of high beauty, and which cast light on the state of the soul after its separation from the body. Her gentle patience with them, her steady reference to a higher cause, her pure joy, when they became

---

3   The women ghosts all wear veils, put on the way admired by the Italian poets, of whom, however, she could know nothing.

white in the light of happiness obtained through aspiration, are worthy of a more than half enfranchised angel.

As to the stories of mental correspondence and visits to those still engaged in this world, such as are told of her presentiment of her father's death, and connexion with him in the last moments, these are probably pure facts. Those who have sufficient strength of affection to be easily disengaged from external impressions and habits, and who dare trust their mental impulses are familiar with such.

Her invention of a language seems a simply natural motion of the mind when left to itself. The language we habitually use is so broken, and so hackneyed by ages of conventional use, that, in all deep states of being, we crave one simple and primitive in its stead. Most persons make one more or less clear from looks, tones, and symbols:--this woman, in the long leisure of her loneliness, and a mind bent upon itself, attempted to compose one of letters and words. I look upon it as no gift from without, but a growth from her own mind.

Her invention of a machine, of which she made a drawing, her power of drawing correctly her life-circle, and sun-circle, and the mathematical feeling she had of her existence, in correspondent sections of the two, are also valuable as mental facts. These figures describe her history and exemplify the position of mathematics toward the world of creative thought.

Every fact of mental existence ought to be capable of similar demonstration. I attach no especial importance to her circles:--we all live in such; all who observe themselves have the same sense of exactness and harmony in the revolutions of their destiny. But few attend to what is simple and invariable in the motions of their minds, and still fewer seek out means clearly to express them to others.

Goethe has taken up these facts in his Wanderjahre, where he speaks of his Macaria; also, one of these persons who are compensated for bodily infirmity by a more concentrated and acute state of mind, and consequent accesses of wisdom, as being bound to a star. When she was engaged by a sense of these larger revolutions, she seemed to those near her on the earth, to be sick; when she was, in fact, lower, but better adapted to the details and variations of an earthly life, these said she was well. Macaria knew the sun and life circles, also, the lives of spirit and soul, as did the forester's daughter of Prevorst.

Her power of making little verses was one of her least gifts. Many excitable persons possess this talent at versification, as all may possess it. It is merely that a certain exaltation of feeling raises the mode of expression with it, in the same way as song differs from speech. Verses of this sort do not necessarily demand the high faculties that constitute the poet,--the creative powers. Many verses, good ones, are personal or national merely. Ballads, hymns, love-lyrics, have often no claim differing from those of common prose speech, to the title of poems, except a greater keenness and terseness of expression.

The verses of this Seherin are of the simplest character, the natural garb for the sighs or aspirations of a lonely heart. She uses the shortest words, the commonest rhymes, and the verses move us by their nature and truth alone.

The most interesting of these facts to me, are her impressions from minerals and plants. Her impressions coincide with many ancient superstitions.

The hazel woke her immediately and gave her more power, therefore the witch with her hazel wand, probably found herself superior to those around her. We may also mention, in reference to witchcraft, that Dr. K. asserts that, in certain moods of mind, she had no weight, but was upborne upon water, like cork, thus confirming the propriety, and justice of our forefathers' ordeal for witchcraft!

The laurel produced on her the highest magnetic effect, therefore the Sibyls had good reasons for wearing it on their brows.

"The laurel had on her, as on most sleep-wakers, a distinguished magnetic effect. We thus see why the priestess at Delphi, previous to uttering her oracles, shook a laurel tree, and then seated herself on a tripod covered with laurel boughs. In the temple of Aesculapius, and others, the laurel was used to excite sleep and dream."

From grapes she declared impressions, which corresponded with those caused by the wines made from them. Many kinds were given her, one after the other, by the person who raised them, and who gives a certificate as to the accuracy of her impressions, and his belief that she could not have derived them from any cause, but that of the touch.

She prescribed vegetable substances to be used in her machine, (as a kind of vapor bath,) and with good results to herself.

She enjoyed contact with minerals, deriving from those she liked a sense of concentrated life. Her impressions of the precious stones, corresponded with many superstitions of the ancients, which led to the preference of certain gems for amu-

Summer on the Lakes

lets, on which they had engraved talismanic figures.

The ancients, in addition to their sense of the qualities that distinguish the diamond above all gems, venerated it as a talisman against wild beasts, poison, and evil spirits, thus expressing the natural influence of what is so enduring, bright, and pure. Townshend, speaking of the effect of gems on one of his sleep-wakers, said, she loved the diamond so much that she would lean her forehead towards it, whenever it was brought near her.

It is observable that these sleep-wakers, in their prescriptions, resemble the ancient sages, who culled only simples for the sick. But if they have this fine sense, also, for the qualities of animal and mineral substances, there is no reason why they should not turn bane to antidote, and prescribe at least homeopathic doses of poison, to restore the diseased to health.

The Seherin ascribed different states to the right and left sides of every body, even of the lady moon. The left is most impressible. Query: Is this the reason why the left hand has been, by the custom of nations, so almost disused, because the heart is on the left side?

She also saw different sights in the left from the right eye. In the left, the bodily state of the person; in the right, his real or destined self, how often unknown to himself, almost always obscured or perverted by his present ignorance or mistake. She had also the gift of second sight. She saw the coffins of those about to die. She saw in mirrors, cups of water; in soap-bubbles, the coming future.

We are here reminded of many beautiful superstitions and legends; of the secret pool in which the daring may, at mid-moon of night, read the future; of the magic globe, on whose pure surface Britomart sees her future love, whom she must seek, arrayed in knightly armor, through a difficult and hostile world.

> A looking-glass, right wondrously aguized,
> Whose virtues through the wyde world soon were solemnized.
> It vertue had to show in perfect sight,
> Whatever thing was in the world contayned,
> Betwixt the lowest earth and hevens hight;
> So that it to the looker appertayned,
> Whatever foe had wrought, or friend had fayned,

Herein discovered was, ne ought mote pas,
 Ne ought in secret from the same remayned;
Forthy it round and hollow shaped was,
Like to the world itselfe, and seemed a World of Glas.

Faerie Queene, Book III.

Such mirrors had Cornelius Agrippa and other wizards. The soap-bubble is such a globe; only one had need of second sight or double sight to see the pictures on so transitory a mirror. Perhaps it is some vague expectation of such wonders, that makes us so fond of blowing them in childish years. But, perhaps, it is rather as a prelude to the occupation of our lives, blowing bubbles where all things may be seen, that, "to the looker appertain," if we can keep them long enough or look quick enough.

In short, were this biography of no other value, it would be most interesting as showing how the floating belief of nations, always no doubt shadowing forth in its imperfect fashion the poetic facts with their scientific exposition, is found to grow up anew in a simple, but high-wrought nature.

The fashioning spirit, working upwards from the clod to man, proffers as its last, highest essay, the brain of man. In the lowest zoophyte it aimed at this; some faint rudiments may there be discerned: but only in man has it perfected that immense galvanic battery that can be loaded from above, below, and around;--that engine, not only of perception, but of conception and consecutive thought,--whose right hand is memory, whose life is idea, the crown of nature, the platform from which spirit takes-wing.

Yet, as gradation is the beautiful secret of nature, and the fashioning spirit, which loves to develop and transcend, loves no less to moderate, to modulate, and harmonize, it did not mean by thus drawing man onward to the next state of existence, to destroy his fitness for this. It did not mean to destroy his sympathies with the mineral, vegetable, and animal realms, of whose components he is in great part composed; which were the preface to his being, of whom he is to take count, whom he should govern as a reasoning head of a perfectly arranged body. He was meant to be the historian, the philosopher, the poet, the king of this world, no less than the prophet of the next.

These functions should be in equipoise, and when they are not, when we see excess either on the natural (so called as distinguished from the spiritual,) or the spiritual side, we feel that the law is transgressed. And, if it be the greatest sorrow to see brain merged in body, to see a man more hands or feet than head, so that we feel he might, with propriety, be on all fours again, or even crawl like the serpent; it is also sad to see the brain, too much excited on some one side, which we call madness, or even unduly and prematurely, so as to destroy in its bloom, the common human existence of the person, as in the case before us, and others of the poetical and prophetical existence.

We would rather minds should foresee less and see more surely, that death should ensue by gentler gradation, and the brain be the governor and interpreter, rather than the destroyer, of the animal life. But, in cases like this, where the animal life is prematurely broken up, and the brain prematurely exercised, we may as well learn what we can from it, and believe that the glimpses thus caught, if not as precious as the full view, are bright with the same light, and open to the same scene.

There is a family character about all the German ghosts. We find the same features in these stories as in those related by Jung Stilling and others. They bear the same character as the pictures by the old masters, of a deep and simple piety. She stands before as, this piety, in a full, high-necked robe, a simple, hausfrauish cap, a clear, straightforward blue eye. These are no terrible, gloomy ghosts with Spanish mantle or Italian dagger. We feel quite at home with them, and sure of their good faith.

To the Seherin, they were a real society, constantly inspiring good thoughts. The reference to them in these verses, written in her journal shortly before her death, is affecting, and shows her deep sense of their reality. She must have felt that she had been a true friend to them, by refusing always, as she did, requests she thought wrong, and referring them to a Saviour.

> Farewell, my friends,
> All farewell,
> God bless you for your love--
> Bless you for your goodness.

>   All farewell!
>
> And you, how shall I name you?
>   Who have so saddened me,
> I will name you also--Friends;
> You have been discipline to me.
>   Farewell! farewell!
>
> Farewell! you my dear ones,
> Soon will you know[4]
> How hard have been my sufferings
>   In the Pilgrim land.
>   Farewell!
>
>   Let it not grieve you,
> That my woes find an end;
>   Farewell, dear ones,
> Till the second meeting;
>   Farewell! Farewell!

In this journal her thoughts dwell much upon those natural ties which she was not permitted to enjoy. She thought much of her children, and often fancied she had saw the one who had died, growing in the spirit land. Any allusion to them called a sweet smile on her face when in her trance.

Other interesting poems are records of these often beautiful visions, especially of that preceding her own death; the address to her life-circle, the thought of which is truly great, (this was translated in the Dublin Magazine,) and descriptions of her earthly state as an imprisonment. The story of her life, though stained like others, by partialities, and prejudices, which were not justly distinguished from what was altogether true and fair, is a poem of so pure a music; presents such gentle and holy

---

4 The physician thought she here referred to the examination of her body that would take place after her death. The brain was found to be sound, though there were marks of great disease elsewhere.

images, that we sympathize fully in the love and gratitude Kerner and his friends felt towards her, as the friend of their best life. She was a St. Theresa in her way.

His address to her, with which his volume closes, may thus be translated in homely guise. In the original it has no merit, except as uttering his affectionate and reverent feeling towards his patient, the peasant girl,--"the sick one, the poor one." But we like to see how, from the mouths of babes and sucklings, praise may be so perfected as to command this reverence from the learned and worldly-wise.

> Farewell; the debt I owe thee
>   Ever in heart I bear;
> My soul sees, since I know thee,
>   The spirit depths so clear.
>
> Whether in light or shade,
>   Thy soul now dwelling hath;
> Be, if my faith should fade,
>   The guide upon my path.
>
> Livest thou in mutual power,
>   With spirits blest and bright,
> O be, in death's dark hour,
>   My help to heaven's light.
>
> Upon thy grave is growing,
>   The plant by thee beloved,[5]
> St. Johns-wort golden glowing,
>   Like St. John's thoughts of love.
>
> Witness of sacred sorrow,
>   Whene'er thou meet'st my eye,
> O flower, from thee I borrow,
>   Thoughts for eternity.

---

5 She received great benefit from decoctions of this herb, and often prescribed it to others.

> Farewell! the woes of earth
> No more my soul affright;
> Who knows their temporal birth
> Can easy bear their weight.

I do confess this is a paraphrase, not a translation, also, that in the other extracts, I have taken liberties with the original for the sake of condensation, and clearness. What I have written must be received as a slight and conversational account, of the work.

Two or three other remarks, I had forgotten, may come in here.

The glances at the spirit-world have none of that large or universal significance, none of that value from philosophical analogy, that is felt in any picture by Swedenborg, or Dante, of permanent relations. The mind of the forester's daughter was exalted and rapidly developed; still the wild cherry tree bore no orange; she was not transformed into a philosophic or poetic organization.

Yet many of her untaught notions remind of other seers of a larger scope. She, too, receives this life as one link in a long chain; and thinks that immediately after death, the meaning of the past life will appear to us as one word.

She tends to a belief in the aromal state, and in successive existences on this earth; for behind persons she often saw another being, whether their form in the state before or after this, I know not; behind a woman a man, equipped for fight, and so forth. Her perception of character, even in cases of those whom she saw only as they passed her window, was correct.

Kerner aims many a leaden sarcasm at those who despise his credulity. He speaks of those sages as men whose brain is a glass table, incapable of receiving the electric spark, and who will not believe, because, in their mental isolation, they are incapable of feeling these facts.

Certainly, I think he would be dull, who could see no meaning or beauty in the history of the forester's daughter of Prevorst. She lived but nine-and-twenty years, yet, in that time, had traversed a larger portion of the field of thought than all her race before, in their many and long lives.

Of the abuses to which all these magical implements are prone, I have an instance, since leaving Milwaukie, in the journal of a man equally sincere, but not equally inspired, led from Germany hither by signs and wonders, as a commissioned agent of Providence, who, indeed, has arranged every detail of his life with a minuteness far beyond the promised care of the sparrow. He props himself by spiritual aid from a maiden now in this country, who was once an attendant on the Seeress, and who seems to have caught from her the contagion of trance, but not its revelations.

Do not blame me that I have written so much about Germany and Hades, while you were looking for news of the West. Here, on the pier, I see disembarking the Germans, the Norwegians, the Swedes, the Swiss. Who knows how much of old legendary lore, of modern wonder, they have already planted amid the Wisconsin forests? Soon, soon their tales of the origin of things, and the Providence which rules them, will be so mingled with those of the Indian, that the very oak trees will not know them apart,--will not know whether itself be a Runic, a Druid, or a Winnebago oak.

Some seeds of all growths that have ever been known in this world might, no doubt, already be found in these Western wilds, if we had the power to call them to life.

I saw, in the newspaper, that the American Tract Society boasted of their agents' having exchanged, at a Western cabin door, tracts for the Devil on Two Sticks, and then burnt that more entertaining than edifying volume. No wonder, though, they study it there. Could one but have the gift of reading the dreams dreamed by men of such various birth, various history, various mind, it would afford much more extensive amusement than did the chambers of one Spanish city!

Could I but have flown at night through such mental experiences, instead of being shut up in my little bedroom at the Milwaukie boarding house, this chapter would have been worth reading. As it is, let us hasten to a close.

Had I been rich in money, I might have built a house, or set up in business, during my fortnight's stay at Milwaukie, matters move on there at so rapid a rate. But, being only rich in curiosity, I was obliged to walk the streets and pick up what I could in casual intercourse. When I left the street, indeed, and walked on the bluffs, or sat beside the lake in their shadow, my mind was rich in dreams congenial to the scene, some time to be realized, though not by me.

A boat was left, keel up, half on the sand, half in the water, swaying with each swell of the lake. It gave a picturesque grace to that part of the shore, as the only image of inaction--only object of a pensive character to be seen. Near this I sat, to dream my dreams and watch the colors of the Jake, changing hourly, till the sun sank. These hours yielded impulses, wove webs, such as life will not again afford.

Returning to the boarding house, which was also a boarding school, we were sure to be greeted by gay laughter.

This school was conducted by two girls of nineteen and seventeen years; their pupils were nearly as old as themselves; the relation seemed very pleasant between them. The only superiority--that of superior knowledge--was sufficient to maintain authority--all the authority that was needed to keep daily life in good order.

In the West, people are not respected merely because they are old in years; people there have not time to keep up appearances in that way; when they cease to have a real advantage in wisdom, knowledge, or enterprise, they must stand back, and let those who are oldest in character "go ahead," however few years they may count. There are no banks of established respectability in which to bury the talent there; no napkin of precedent in which to wrap it. What cannot be made to pass current, is not esteemed coin of the realm.

To the windows of this house, where the daughter of a famous "Indian fighter," i.e. fighter against the Indians, was learning French and the piano, came wild, tawny figures, offering for sale their baskets of berries. The boys now, instead of brandishing the tomahawk, tame their hands to pick raspberries.

Here the evenings were much lightened by the gay chat of one of the party, who, with the excellent practical sense of mature experience, and the kindest heart, united a naivete and innocence such as I never saw in any other who had walked so long life's tangled path. Like a child, she was everywhere at home, and like a child, received and bestowed entertainment from all places, all persons. I thanked her for making me laugh, as did the sick and poor, whom she was sure to find out in her briefest sojourn in any place, for more substantial aid. Happy are those who never grieve, and so often aid and enliven their fellow men!

This scene, however, I was not sorry to exchange for the much celebrated beauties of the Island of Mackinaw.

CHAPTER VI.
MACKINAW.

Late at night we reached this island, so famous for its beauty, and to which I proposed a visit of some length. It was the last week in August, when a large representation from the Chippewa and Ottowa tribes are here to receive their annual payments from the American government. As their habits make travelling easy and inexpensive to them, neither being obliged to wait for steamboats, or write to see whether hotels are full, they come hither by thousands, and those thousands in families, secure of accommodation on the beach, and food from the lake, to make a long holiday out of the occasion. There were near two thousand encamped on the island already, and more arriving every day.

As our boat came in, the captain had some rockets let off. This greatly excited the Indians, and their yells and wild cries resounded along the shore. Except for the momentary flash of the rockets, it was perfectly dark, and my sensations as I walked with a stranger to a strange hotel, through the midst of these shrieking savages, and heard the pants and snorts of the departing steamer, which carried away all my companions, were somewhat of the dismal sort; though it was pleasant, too, in the way that everything strange is; everything that breaks in upon the routine that so easily incrusts us.

I had reason to expect a room to myself at the hotel, but found none, and was obliged to take up my rest in the common parlor and eating-room, a circumstance which ensured my being an early riser.

With the first rosy streak, I was out among my Indian neighbors, whose lodges honey-combed the beautiful beach, that curved away in long, fair outline on either side the house. They were already on the alert, the children creeping out from beneath the blanket door of the lodge; the women pounding corn in their rude mortars, the young men playing on their pipes. I had been much amused, when the strain proper to the Winnebago courting flute was played to me on another instrument, at any one fancying it a melody; but now, when I heard the notes in their true tone and time, I thought it not unworthy comparison, in its graceful sequence, and the light flourish, at the close, with the sweetest bird-songs; and this, like the bird-song, is only practised to allure a mate. The Indian, become a citizen and a husband, no more thinks of playing the flute than one of the "settled down" members of our society would of choosing the "purple light of love" as dye-stuff for a surtout.

Mackinaw has been fully described by able pens, and I can only add my tribute to the exceeding beauty of the spot and its position. It is charming to be on an island so small that you can sail round it in an afternoon, yet large enough to admit of long secluded walks through its gentle groves. You can go round it in your boat; or, on foot, you can tread its narrow beach, resting, at times, beneath the lofty walls of stone, richly wooded, which rise from it in various architectural forms. In this stone, caves are continually forming, from the action of the atmosphere; one of these is quite deep, and with a fragment left at its mouth, wreathed with little creeping plants, that looks, as you sit within, like a ruined pillar.

The arched rock surprised me, much as I had heard of it, from the perfection of the arch. It is perfect whether you look up through it from the lake, or down through it to the transparent waters. We both ascended and descended, no very easy matter, the steep and crumbling path, and rested at the summit, beneath the trees, and at the foot upon the cool mossy stones beside the lapsing wave. Nature has carefully decorated all this architecture with shrubs that take root within the crevices, and small creeping vines. These natural rains may vie for beautiful effect with the remains of European grandeur, and have, beside, a charm as of a playful mood in nature.

The sugar-loaf rock is a fragment in the same kind as the pine rock we saw in Illinois. It has the same air of a helmet, as seen from an eminence at the side, which you descend by a long and steep path. The rock itself may be ascended by the bold and agile. Halfway up is a niche, to which those, who are neither, can climb by a ladder. A very handsome young officer and lady who were with us did so, and then, facing round, stood there side by side, looking in the niche, if not like saints or angels wrought by pious hands in stone, as romantically, if not as holily, worthy the gazer's eye.

The woods which adorn the central ridge of the island are very full in foliage, and, in August, showed the tender green and pliant leaf of June elsewhere. They are rich in beautiful mosses and the wild raspberry.

From Fort Holmes, the old fort, we had the most commanding view of the lake and straits, opposite shores, and fair islets. Mackinaw, itself, is best seen from the water. Its peculiar shape is supposed to have been the origin of its name, Michilimackinac, which means the Great Turtle. One person whom I saw, wished to establish another etymology, which he fancied to be more refined; but, I doubt not, this is the true one, both because the shape might suggest such a name, and that the existence of an island in this commanding position, which did so, would seem a significant fact to the Indians. For Henry gives the details of peculiar worship paid to the Great Turtle, and the oracles received from this extraordinary Apollo of the Indian Delphos.

It is crowned most picturesquely, by the white fort, with its gay flag. From this, on one side, stretches the town. How pleasing a sight, after the raw, crude, staring assemblage of houses, everywhere else to be met in this country, an old French town, mellow in its coloring, and with the harmonious effect of a slow growth, which assimilates, naturally, with objects round it. The people in its streets, Indian, French, half-breeds, and others, walked with a leisure step, as of those who live a life of taste and inclination, rather than of the hard press of business, as in American towns elsewhere.

On the other side, along the fair, curving beach, below the white houses scattered on the declivity, clustered the Indian lodges, with their amber brown matting, so soft, and bright of hue, in the late afternoon sun. The first afternoon I was there, looking down from a near height, I felt that I never wished to see a more fascinating picture. It was an hour of the deepest serenity; bright blue and gold, rich shadows. Every moment the sunlight fell more mellow. The Indians were grouped and scattered among the lodges; the women preparing food, in the kettle or frying-pan, over the many small fires; the children, half-naked, wild as little goblins, were playing both in and out of the water. Here and there lounged a young girl, with a baby at her back, whose bright eyes glanced, as if born into a world of courage and of joy, instead of ignominious servitude and slow decay. Some girls were cutting wood, a little way from me, talking and laughing, in the low musical tone, so charming in the Indian women. Many bark canoes were upturned upon the beach, and, by that light, of almost the same amber as the lodges. Others, coming in, their square sails set, and with almost arrowy speed, though heavily laden with dusky forms, and all the apparatus of their household. Here and there a sail-boat glided by, with a different, but scarce less pleasing motion.

It was a scene of ideal loveliness, and these wild forms adorned it, as looking so at home in it. All seemed happy, and they were happy that day, for they had no firewater to madden them, as it was Sunday, and the shops were shut.

From my window, at the boarding house, my eye was constantly attracted by these picturesque groups. I was never tired of seeing the canoes come in, and the new arrivals set up their temporary dwellings. The women ran to set up the tent-poles, and spread the mats on the ground. The men brought the chests, kettles, &c.; the mats were then laid on the outside, the cedar boughs strewed on the ground, the blanket hung up for a door, and all was completed in less than twenty minutes. Then they began to prepare the night meal, and to learn of their neighbors the news of the day.

The habit of preparing food out of doors, gave all the gipsy charm and variety to their conduct. Continually I wanted Sir. Walter Scott to have been there. If such romantic sketches were suggested to him, by the sight of a few gipsies, not a group near one of these fires but would have furnished him material for a separate canvass. I was so taken up with the spirit of the scene, that I could not follow out the stories suggested by these weather-beaten, sullen, but eloquent figures.

They talked a great deal, and with much variety of gesture, so that I often had a good guess at the meaning of their discourse. I saw that, whatever the Indian may be among the whites, he is anything but taciturn with his own people. And he often would declaim, or narrate at length, as indeed it is obvious, that these tribes possess great power that way, if only from the fables taken from their stores, by Mr. Schoolcraft.

I liked very much to walk or sit among them. With the women I held much communication by signs. They are almost invariably coarse and ugly, with the exception of their eyes, with a peculiarly awkward gait, and forms bent by burthens. This gait, so different from the steady and noble step of the men, marks the inferior position they occupy. I had heard much eloquent contradiction of this. Mrs. Schoolcraft had maintained to a friend, that they were in fact as nearly on a par with their husbands as the white woman with hers. "Although," said she, "on account of inevitable causes, the Indian woman is subjected to many hardships of a peculiar nature, yet her position, compared with that of the man, is higher and freer than that of the white woman. Why will people look only on one side? They either exalt the Red man into a Demigod or degrade him into a beast. They say that he compels his wife to do all the drudgery, while he does nothing but hunt and amuse himself; forgetting that, upon his activity and power of endurance as a hunter, depends the support of his family; that this is labor of the most fatiguing kind, and that it is absolutely necessary that he should keep his frame unbent by burdens and unworn by toil, that he may be able to obtain the means of subsistence. I have witnessed scenes of conjugal and parental love in the Indian's wigwam from which I have often, often thought the educated white man, proud of his superior civilization, might learn an useful lesson. When he returns from hunting, worn out with fatigue, having tasted nothing since dawn, his wife, if she is a good wife, will take off his moccasons and replace them with dry ones, and will prepare his game for their repast, while his children will climb upon him, and he will caress them with all the tenderness of a woman; and in the evening the Indian wigwam is the scene of the purest domestic pleasures. The father will relate for the amusement of the wife, and for the instruction of the children, all the events of the day's hunt, while they will treasure up every word that falls, and thus learn the theory of the art, whose practice is to be the occupation of their lives.

Mrs. Grant speaks thus of the position of woman amid the Mohawk Indians:

"Lady Mary Montague says, that the court of Vienna was the paradise of old women, and that there is no other place in the world where a woman past fifty excites the least interest. Had her travels extended to the interior of North America, she would have seen another instance of this inversion of the common mode of thinking. Here a woman never was of consequence, till she had a son old enough to fight the battles of his country. From that date she held a superior rank in society; was allowed to live at ease, and even called to consultations on national affairs. In savage and warlike countries, the reign of beauty is very short, and its influence comparatively limited. The girls in childhood had a very pleasing appearance; but excepting their fine hair, eyes, and teeth, every external grace was soon banished by perpetual drudgery, carrying burdens too heavy to be borne, and other slavish employments considered beneath the dignity of the men. These walked before erect and graceful, decked with ornaments which set off to advantage the symmetry of their well-formed persons, while the poor women followed, meanly attired, bent under the weight of the children and utensils, which they carried everywhere with them, and disfigured and degraded by ceaseless toils. They were very early married, for a Mohawk had no other servant but his wife, and, whenever he commenced hunter, it was requisite he should have some one to carry his load, cook his kettle, make his moccasons, and, above all, produce the young warriors who were to succeed him in the honors of the chase and of the tomahawk. Wherever man is a mere hunter, woman is a mere slave. It is domestic intercourse that softens man, and elevates woman; and of that there can be but little, where the employments and amusements are not in common; the ancient Caledonians honored the fair; but then it is to be observed, they were fair huntresses, and moved in the light of their beauty to the hill of roes; and the culinary toils were entirely left to the rougher sex. When the young warrior made his appearance, it softened the cares of his mother, who well knew that, when he grew up, every deficiency in tenderness to his wife would be made up in superabundant duty and affection to her. If it were possible to carry filial veneration to excess, it was done here; for all other charities were absorbed in it. I wonder this system of depressing the sex in their early years, to exalt them when all their juvenile attractions were flown, and when mind alone can distinguish them, has not occurred to our modern reformers. The Mohawks took good care not to admit their women to share their prerogatives, till they approved themselves good wives and mothers."

The observations of women upon the position of woman are always more valuable than those of men; but, of these two, Mrs. Grant's seems much nearer the truth than Mrs. Schoolcraft's, because, though her opportunities for observation did not bring her so close, she looked more at both sides to find the truth.

Carver, in his travels among the Winnebagoes, describes two queens, one nominally so, like Queen Victoria; the other invested with a genuine royalty, springing from her own conduct.

In the great town of the Winnebagoes, he found a queen presiding over the tribe, instead of a sachem. He adds, that, in some tribes, the descent is given to the female line in preference to the male, that is, a sister's son will succeed to the authority, rather than a brother's son.

The position of this Winnebago queen, reminded me forcibly of Queen Victoria's.

"She sat in the council, but only asked a few questions, or gave some trifling directions in matters relative to the state, for women are never allowed to sit in their councils, except they happen to be invested with the supreme authority, and then it is not customary for them to make any formal speeches, as the chiefs do. She was a very ancient woman, small in stature, and not much distinguished by her dress from several young women that attended her. These, her attendants, seemed greatly pleased whenever I showed any tokens of respect to their queen, especially when I saluted her, which I frequently did to acquire her favor."

The other was a woman, who being taken captive, found means to kill her captor, and make her escape, and the tribe were so struck with admiration at the courage and calmness she displayed on the occasion, as to make her chieftainess in her own right.

Notwithstanding the homage paid to women, and the consequence allowed her in some cases, it is impossible to look upon the Indian women, without feeling that they ***do*** occupy a lower place than women among the nations of European civilization. The habits of drudgery expressed in their form and gesture, the soft and wild but melancholy expression of their eye, reminded me of the tribe mentioned by Mackenzie, where the women destroy their female children, whenever they have a good opportunity; and of the eloquent reproaches addressed by the Paraguay woman to her mother, that she had not, in the same way, saved her from the anguish and weariness of her lot.

More weariness than anguish, no doubt, falls to the lot of most of these women. They inherit submission, and the minds of the generality accommodate themselves more or less to any posture. Perhaps they suffer less than their white sisters, who have more aspiration and refinement, with little power of self-sustenance. But their place is certainly lower, and their share of the human inheritance less.

Their decorum and delicacy are striking, and show that when these are native to the mind, no habits of life make any difference. Their whole gesture is timid, yet self-possessed. They used to crowd round me, to inspect little things I had to show them, but never press near; on the contrary, would reprove and keep off the children. Anything they took from my hand, was held with care, then shut or folded, and returned with an air of lady-like precision. They would not stare, however curious they might be, but cast sidelong glances.

A locket that I wore, was an object of untiring interest; they seemed to regard it as a talisman. My little sun-shade was still more fascinating to them; apparently they had never before seen one. For an umbrella they entertain profound regard, probably looking upon it as the most luxurious superfluity a person can possess, and therefore a badge of great wealth. I used to see an old squaw, whose sullied skin and coarse, tanned locks, told that she had braved sun and storm, without a doubt or care, for sixty years at the least, sitting gravely at the door of her lodge, with an old green umbrella over her head, happy for hours together in the dignified shade. For her happiness pomp came not, as it so often does, too late; she received it with grateful enjoyment.

One day, as I was seated on one of the canoes, a woman came and sat beside me, with her baby in its cradle set up at her feet. She asked me by a gesture, to let her take my sun-shade, and then to show her how to open it. Then she put it into her baby's hand, and held it over its head, looking at me the while with a sweet, mischievous laugh, as much as to say, "you carry a thing that is only fit for a baby;" her pantomime was very pretty. She, like the other women, had a glance, and shy, sweet expression in the eye; the men have a steady gaze.

That noblest and loveliest of modern Preux, Lord Edward Fitzgerald, who came through Buffalo to Detroit and Mackinaw, with Brant, and was adopted into the Bear tribe by the name of Eghnidal, was struck, in the same way, by the delicacy of manners in the women. He says, "Notwithstanding the life they lead, which would make most women rough and masculine, they are as soft, meek and modest, as the best brought up girls in England. Somewhat coquettish too! Imagine the manners of Mimi in a poor *squaw*, that has been carrying packs in the woods all her life."

McKenney mentions that the young wife, during the short bloom of her beauty, is an object of homage and tenderness to her husband. One Indian woman, the Flying Pigeon, a beautiful, an excellent woman, of whom he gives some particulars, is an instance of the power uncommon characters will always exert of breaking down the barriers custom has erected round them. She captivated by her charms, and inspired with reverence for her character, her husband and son. The simple praise with which the husband indicates the religion, the judgment, and the generosity he saw in her, are as satisfying as Count Zinzendorf's more labored eulogium on his "noble consort." The conduct of her son, when, many years after her death, he saw her picture at Washington, is unspeakably affecting. Catlin gives anecdotes of the grief of a chief for the loss of a daughter, and the princely gifts he offers in exchange for her portrait, worthy not merely of European, but of Troubadour sentiment. It is also evident that, as Mrs. Schoolcraft says, the women have great power at home. It can never be otherwise, men being dependent upon them for the comfort of their lives. Just, so among ourselves, wives who are neither esteemed nor loved by their husbands, have great power over their conduct by the friction of every day, and over the formation of their opinions by the daily opportunities so close a relation affords, of perverting testimony and instilling doubts. But these sentiments should not come in brief flashes, but burn as a steady flame, then there would be more women worthy to inspire them. This power is good for nothing, unless the woman be wise to use it aright. Has the Indian, has the white woman, as noble a feeling of life and its uses, as religious a self-respect, as worthy a field of thought and action, as man? If not, the white woman, the Indian woman, occupies an inferior position to that of man. It is not so much a question of power, as of privilege.

The men of these subjugated tribes, now accustomed to drunkenness and every way degraded, bear but a faint impress of the lost grandeur of the race. They are no longer strong, tall, or finely proportioned. Yet as you see them stealing along a height, or striding boldly forward, they remind you of what *was* majestic in the red man.

On the shores of lake Superior, it is said, if you visit them at home, you may still see a remnant of the noble blood. The Pillagers--(Pilleurs)--a band celebrated by the old travellers, are: still existant there.

"Still some, 'the eagles of their tribe,' may rush."

I have spoken of the hatred felt by the white man for the Indian: with white women it seems to amount to disgust, to loathing. How I could endure the dirt, the peculiar smell of the Indians, and their dwellings, was a great marvel in the eyes of my lady acquaintance; indeed, I wonder why they did not quite give me up, as they certainly looked on me with great distaste for it. "Get you gone, you Indian dog," was the felt, if not the breathed, expression towards the hapless owners of the soil. All their claims, all their sorrows quite forgot, in abhorrence of their dirt, their tawny skins, and the vices the whites have taught them.

A person who had seen them during great part of a life, expressed his prejudices to me with such violence, that I was no longer surprised that the Indian children threw sticks at him, as he passed. A lady said, "do what you will for them, they will be ungrateful. The savage cannot be washed out of them. Bring up an Indian child and see if you can attach it to you." The next moment, she expressed, in the presence of one of those children whom she was bringing up, loathing at the odor left by one of her people, and one of the most respected, as he passed through the room. When the child is grown she will consider it basely ungrateful not to love her, as it certainly will not; and this will be cited as an instance of the impossibility of attaching the Indian.

Whether the Indian could, by any efforts of love and intelligence from the white man, have been civilized and made a valuable ingredient in the new state, I will not say; but this we are sure of; the French Catholics, at least, did not harm them, nor disturb their minds merely to corrupt them. The French they loved. But the stern Presbyterian, with his dogmas and his task-work, the city circle and the college, with their niggard concessions and unfeeling stare, have never tried the experiment. It has not been tried. Our people and our government have sinned alike against the first-born of the soil, and if they are the fated agents of a new era, they have done nothing--have invoked no god to keep them sinless while they do the hest of fate.

Worst of all, when they invoke the holy power only to mask their iniquity; when the felon trader, who, all the week, has been besotting and degrading the Indian with rum mixed with red pepper, and damaged tobacco, kneels with him on Sunday before a common altar, to tell the rosary which recalls the thought of him crucified for love of suffering men, and to listen to sermons in praise of "purity"!!

My savage friends, cries the old fat priest, you must, above all things, aim at *purity*.

Oh, my heart swelled when I saw them in a Christian church. Better their own dog-feasts and bloody rites than such mockery of that other faith.

"The dog," said an Indian, "was once a spirit; he has fallen for his sin, and was given by the Great Spirit, in this shape, to man, as his most intelligent companion. Therefore we sacrifice it in highest honor to our friends in this world,--to our protecting geniuses in another."

There was religion in that thought. The white man sacrifices his own brother, and to Mammon, yet he turns in loathing from the dog-feast.

"You say," said the Indian of the South to the missionary, "that Christianity is pleasing to God. How can that be?--Those men at Savannah are Christians."

Yes! slave-drivers and Indian traders are called Christians, and the Indian is to be deemed less like the Son of Mary than they! Wonderful is the deceit of man's heart!

I have not, on seeing something of them in their own haunts, found reason to change the sentiments expressed in the following lines, when a deputation of the Sacs and Foxes visited Boston in 1837, and were, by one person at least, received in a dignified and courteous manner.

GOVERNOR EVERETT RECEIVING THE INDIAN CHIEFS,

NOVEMBER, 1837.

Who says that Poesy is on the wane,
And that the Muses tune their lyres in vain?
'Mid all the treasures of romantic story,
When thought was fresh and fancy in her glory,
Has ever Art found out a richer theme,
More dark a shadow, or more soft a gleam,
Than fall upon the scene, sketched carelessly,
In the newspaper column of to-day?

American romance is somewhat stale.
Talk of the hatchet, and the faces pale,
Wampum and calumets and forests dreary,
Once so attractive, now begins to weary.

Uncas and Magawisca please us still,
Unreal, yet idealized with skill;
But every poetaster scribbling witling,
From the majestic oak his stylus whittling,
Has helped to tire us, and to make us fear
The monotone in which so much we hear
Of "stoics of the wood," and "men without a tear."

Yet Nature, ever buoyant, ever young,
If let alone, will sing as erst she sung;
The course of circumstance gives back again
The Picturesque, erewhile pursued in vain;
Shows us the fount of Romance is not wasted--
The lights and shades of contrast not exhausted.

Shorn of his strength, the Samson now must sue
  For fragments from the feast his fathers gave,
The Indian dare not claim what is his due,
  But as a boon his heritage must crave;
His stately form shall soon be seen no more
Through all his father's land, th' Atlantic shore,
Beneath the sun, to **us** so kind, **they** melt,
More heavily each day our rule is felt;
The tale is old,--we do as mortals must:
Might makes right here, but God and Time are just.

So near the drama hastens to its close,
On this last scene awhile your eyes repose;
The polished Greek and Scythian meet again,
The ancient life is lived by modern men--
The savage through our busy cities walks,--
He in his untouched grandeur silent stalks.
Unmoved by all our gaieties and shows,

Wonder nor shame can touch him as he goes;
He gazes on the marvels we have wrought,
But knows the models from whence all was brought;
In God's first temples he has stood so oft,
And listened to the natural organ loft--
Has watched the eagle's flight, the muttering thunder heard,
Art cannot move him to a wondering word;
Perhaps he sees that all this luxury
Brings less food to the mind than to the eye;
Perhaps a simple sentiment has brought
More to him than your arts had ever taught.
What are the petty triumphs *Art* has given,
To eyes familiar with the naked heaven?

All has been seen--dock, railroad, and canal,
Fort, market, bridge, college, and arsenal,
Asylum, hospital, and cotton mill,
The theatre, the lighthouse, and the jail.
The Braves each novelty, reflecting, saw,
And now and then growled out the earnest *yaw*.
And now the time is come, 'tis understood,
When, having seen and thought so much, a *talk* may do some good.

A well-dressed mob have thronged the sight to greet,
And motley figures throng the spacious street;
Majestical and calm through all they stride,
Wearing the blanket with a monarch's pride;
The gazers stare and shrug, but can't deny
Their noble forms and blameless symmetry.
If the Great Spirit their morale has slighted,
And wigwam smoke their mental culture blighted,
Yet the physique, at least, perfection reaches,
In wilds where neither Combe nor Spursheim teaches;

Where whispering trees invite man to the chase,
And bounding deer allure him to the race.

Would thou hadst seen it! That dark, stately band,
Whose ancestors enjoyed all this fair land,
Whence they, by force or fraud, were made to flee,
Are brought, the white man's victory to see.
Can kind emotions in their proud hearts glow,
As through these realms, now decked by Art, they go?
The church, the school, the railroad and the mart--
Can these a pleasure to their minds impart?
All once was theirs--earth, ocean, forest, sky--
How can they joy in what now meets the eye?
Not yet Religion has unlocked the soul,
Nor Each has learned to glory in the Whole!

Must they not think, so strange and sad their lot,
That they by the Great Spirit are forgot?
From the far border to which they are driven,
They might look up in trust to the clear heaven;
But *here*--what tales doth every object tell
Where Massasoit sleeps--where Philip fell!

We take our turn, and the Philosopher
Sees through the clouds a hand which cannot err,
An unimproving race, with all their graces
And all their vices, must resign their places;
And Human Culture rolls its onward flood
Over the broad plains steeped in Indian blood.
Such thoughts, steady our faith; yet there will rise
Some natural tears into the calmest eyes--
Which gaze where forest princes haughty go,
Made for a gaping crowd a raree show.

But *this* a scene seems where, in courtesy,
The pale face with the forest prince could vie,
For One presided, who, for tact and grace,
In any age had held an honored place,--
In Beauty's own dear day, had shone a polished Phidian vase!

Oft have I listened to his accents bland,
  And owned the magic of his silvery voice,
In all the graces which life's arts demand,
  Delighted by the justness of his choice.
Not his the stream of lavish, fervid thought,--
The rhetoric by passion's magic wrought;
Not his the massive style, the lion port,
Which with the granite class of mind assort;
But, in a range of excellence his own,
With all the charms to soft persuasion known,
Amid our busy people we admire him--"elegant and lone."

He scarce needs words, so exquisite the skill
Which modulates the tones to do his will,
That the mere sound enough would charm the ear,
And lap in its Elysium all who hear.
The intellectual paleness of his cheek,
  The heavy eyelids and slow, tranquil smile,
The well cut lips from which the graces speak,
  Fit him alike to win or to beguile;
Then those words so well chosen, fit, though few,
Their linked sweetness as our thoughts pursue,
We deem them spoken pearls, or radiant diamond dew.

And never yet did I admire the power
  Which makes so lustrous every threadbare theme--
Which won for Lafayette one other hour,

And e'en on July Fourth could cast a gleam--
As now, when I behold him play the host,
With all the dignity which red men boast--
With all the courtesy the whites have lost;--
Assume the very hue of savage mind,
Yet in rude accents show the thought refined:--
Assume the naivete of infant age,
And in such prattle seem still more a sage;
The golden mean with tact unerring seized,
A courtly critic shone, a simple savage pleased;
The stoic of the woods his skill confessed,
As all the Father answered in his breast,
To the sure mark the silver arrow sped,
The man without a tear a tear has shed;
And thou hadst wept, hadst thou been there, to see
How true one sentiment must ever be,
In court or camp, the city or the wild,
To rouse the Father's heart, you need but name his Child.

'Twas a fair scene--and acted well by all;
So here's a health to Indian braves so tall--
Our Governor and Boston people all!

I will copy the admirable speech of Governor Everett on that occasion, as I think it the happiest attempt ever made to meet the Indian in his own way, and catch the tone of his mind. It was said, in the newspapers, that Keokuck did actually shed tears when addressed as a father. If he did not with his eyes, he well might in his heart.

EVERETT'S SPEECH.

Chiefs and warriors of the Sauks and Foxes, you are welcome to our hall of council.

Brothers! you have come a long way from home to visit your white brethren; we rejoice to take you by the hand.

Brothers! we have heard the names of your chiefs and warriors; our brothers, who have travelled into the West, have told us a great deal of the Sauks and Foxes; we rejoice to see you with our own eyes, and take you by the hand.

Brothers! we are called the Massachusetts. This is the name of the red men that once lived here. Their wigwams filled yonder field; their council fire was kindled on this spot. They were of the same great race as the Sauks and Misquakuiks.

Brothers! when our fathers came over the great waters, they were a small band. The red man stood upon the rock by the seaside, and saw our fathers. He might have pushed them into the water and drowned them. But he stretched out his arm to our fathers and said, "Welcome, white men!" Our fathers were hungry, and the red men gave them corn and venison. Our fathers were cold, and the red man wrapped them up in his blanket. We are now numerous and powerful, but we remember the kindness of the red man to our fathers. Brothers, you are welcome; we are glad to see you.

Brothers! our faces are pale, and your faces are dark; but our hearts are alike. The Great Spirit has made his children of different colors, but he loves them all.

Brothers! you dwell between the Mississippi and the Missouri. They are mighty rivers. They have one branch far East in the Alleghanies, and the other far West in the Rocky Mountains; but they flow together at last into one great stream, and run down together into the sea. In like manner, the red man dwells in the West, and the white man in the East, by the great waters; but they are all one branch, one family; it has many branches and one head.

Brothers! as you entered our council house, you beheld the image of our great Father Washington. It is a cold stone--it cannot speak. But he was the friend of the red man, and bad his children live in peace with their red brethren. He is gone to the world of spirits. But his words have made a very deep print in our hearts, like the step of a strong buffalo on the soft clay of the prairie.

Brother! I perceive your little son between your knees. God preserve his life, my brother. He grows up before you like the tender sapling by the side of the mighty oak. May the oak and the sapling flourish a long time together. And when the mighty oak is fallen to the ground, may the young tree fill its place in the forest, and spread out its branches over the tribe like the parent trunk.

Brothers! I make you a short talk, and again bid you welcome to our council hall.

Not often have they been addressed with such intelligence and tact. The few who have not approached them with sordid rapacity, but from love to them, as men, and souls to be redeemed, have most frequently been persons intellectually too narrow, too straightly bound in sects or opinions, to throw themselves into the character or position of the Indians, or impart to them anything they can make available. The Christ shown them by these missionaries, is to them but a new and more powerful Manito; the signs of the new religion, but the fetiches that have aided the conquerors.

Here I will copy some remarks made by a discerning observer, on the methods used by the missionaries, and their natural results.

"Mr. ---- and myself had a very interesting conversation, upon the subject of the Indians, their character, capabilities, &c. After ten years' experience among them, he was forced to acknowledge, that the results of the missionary efforts had produced nothing calculated to encourage. He thought that there was an intrinsic disability in them, to rise above, or go beyond the sphere in which they had so long moved. He said, that even those Indians who had been converted, and who had adopted the habits of civilization, were very little improved in their real character; they were as selfish, as deceitful, and as indolent, as those who were still heathens. They had repaid the kindnesses of the missionaries with the basest ingratitude, killing their cattle and swine, and robbing them of their harvests, which they wantonly destroyed. He had abandoned the idea of effecting any general good to the Indians. He had conscientious scruples, as to promoting an enterprise so hopeless, as that of missions among the Indians, by sending accounts to the east, that might induce philanthropic individuals to contribute to their support. In fact, the whole experience of his intercourse with them, seemed to have convinced him of the irremediable degradation of the race. Their fortitude under suffering, he considered the result of physical and mental insensibility; their courage, a mere animal excitement, which they found it necessary to inflame, before daring to meet a foe. They have no constancy of purpose; and are, in fact, but little superior to the brutes, in point of moral development. It is not astonishing, that one looking upon the Indian character, from Mr. ----'s point of view, should entertain such sentiments. The object of his intercourse with them was, to make them apprehend the mysteries of a theology, which, to the most enlightened, is an abstruse, metaphysical study; and it is not singular they should prefer their pagan superstitions, which address themselves more directly to the senses. Failing in the attempt to christianize, before civilizing them, he inferred, that, in the intrinsic degradation of their faculties, the obstacle was to be found."

Thus the missionary vainly attempts, by once or twice holding up the cross, to turn deer and tigers into lambs; vainly attempts to convince the red man that a heavenly mandate takes from him his broad lands. He bows his head, but does not at heart acquiesce. He cannot. It is not true; and if it were, the descent of blood through the same channels, for centuries, had formed habits of thought not so easily to be disturbed.

Amalgamation would afford the only true and profound means of civilization. But nature seems, like all else, to declare, that this race is fated to perish. Those of mixed blood fade early, and are not generally a fine race. They lose what is best in either type, rather than enhance the value of each, by mingling. There are exceptions, one or two such I know of, but this, it is said, is the general rule.

A traveller observes, that the white settlers, who live in the woods, soon become sallow, lanky, and dejected; the atmosphere of the trees does not agree with Caucasian lungs; and it is, perhaps, in part, an instinct of this, which causes the hatred of the new settlers towards trees. The Indian breathed the atmosphere of the forests freely; he loved their shade. As they are effaced from the land, he fleets too; a part of the same manifestation, which cannot linger behind its proper era.

The Chippewas have lately petitioned the state of Michigan, that they may be admitted as citizens; but this would be vain, unless they could be admitted, as brothers, to the heart of the white man. And while the latter feels that conviction of superiority, which enabled our Wisconsin friend to throw away the gun, and send the Indian to fetch it, he had need to be very good, and very wise, not to abuse his position. But the white man, as yet, is a half-tamed pirate, and avails himself, as much as ever, of the maxim, "Might makes right." All that civilization does for the generality, is to cover up this with a veil of subtle evasions and chicane, and here and there to rouse the individual mind to appeal to heaven against it.

I have no hope of liberalizing the missionary, of humanizing the sharks of trade, of infusing the conscientious drop into the flinty bosom of policy, of saving the Indian from immediate degradation, and speedy death. The, whole sermon may be preached from the text, "Needs be that offences must come, yet we them by whom they come." Yet, ere they depart, I wish there might be some masterly attempt to reproduce, in art or literature, what is proper to them, a kind of beauty and grandeur, which few of the every-day crowd have hearts to feel, yet which ought to leave in the world its monuments, to inspire the thought of genius through all ages. Nothing in this kind has been done masterly; since it was Clevengers's ambition, 'tis pity he had not opportunity to try fully his powers. We hope some other mind may be bent upon it, ere too late.

At present the only lively impress of their passage through the world is to be found in such books as Catlin's and some stories told by the old travellers, of which I purpose a brief account.

First, let me give another brief tale of the power exerted by the white man over the savage in a trying case, but, in this case, it was righteous, was moral power.

"We were looking over McKenney's trip to the Lakes, and, on observing the picture of Key-way-no-wut, or the Going Cloud, Mr. B. observed "Ah, that is the fellow I came near having a fight with," and he detailed at length the circumstances. This Indian was a very desperate character, and whom all the Leech lake band stood in fear of. He would shoot down any Indian who offended him, without the least hesitation, and had become quite the bully of that part of the tribe. The trader at Leech lake warned Mr. B. to beware of him, and said that he once, when he (the trader) refused to give up to him his stock of wild rice, went and got his gun and tomahawk, and shook the tomahawk over his head, saying "Now, give me your wild rice." The trader complied with his exaction, but not so did Mr. B. in the adventure which I am about to relate. Key-way-no-wut came frequently to him with furs, wishing him to give for them cotton cloth, sugar, flour, &c. Mr. B. explained to him that he could not trade for furs, as he was sent there as a teacher, and that it would be like putting his hand into the fire to do so, as the traders would inform against him, and he would be sent out of the country. At the same time, he ***gave*** him the articles which he wished. Key-way-no-wut found this a very convenient way of getting what he wanted, and followed up this sort of game, until, at last, it became insupportable. One day the Indian brought a very large otter skin, and said "I want to get for this ten pounds of sugar, and some flour and cloth," adding, "I am not like other Indians, ***I*** want to pay for what I get. Mr. B. found that he must either be robbed of all he had by submitting to these exactions, or take a stand at once. He thought, however, he would try to avoid a scrape, and told his customer he had not so much sugar to spare. "Give me then," said he, "what you can spare," and Mr. B. thinking to make him back out, told him he would give him five pounds of sugar for his skin. "Take it," said the Indian. He left the skin, telling Mr. B. to take good care of it. Mr. B. took it at once to the trader's store, and related the circumstance, congratulating himself that he had got rid of the Indian's exactions. But, in about a month, Key-way-no-wut appeared bringing some dirty Indian sugar, and said "I have brought back the sugar that I borrowed of you, and I want my otter skin back." Mr. B. told him, "I ***bought*** an otter skin of you, but if you will return the other articles you have got for it, perhaps I can get it for you." "Where is the skin?" said he very quickly, "what have you done with it?" Mr. B. replied it was in the trader's store, where he (the Indian) could not get it. At this information he was furious, laid his hands on his knife and tomahawk, and commanded Mr. B. to bring it at once. Mr. B. found this was the crisis, where he must take a stand or be "rode over rough shod" by this man; his wife, who was present was much alarmed, and begged he would get the skin for the Indian, but he told her that "either he or the Indian would soon be master of his house, and if she was afraid to see it decided which was to be so, she had better retire." He turned to Key-way-no-wut, and addressed him in a stern voice as follows: "I will ***not*** give you the skin. How often have you come to my house, and I have shared with you what I had. I gave you tobacco when you were well, and medicine when you were sick, and you never went away from my wigwam with your hands empty. And this is the way you return my treatment to you. I had thought you were a man and a chief, but you are not, you are nothing but an old woman. Leave this house, and never enter it again." Mr. B. said he expected the Indian would attempt his life when he said this, but that he had placed himself in a position so that he could defend himself, and he looked straight into the Indian's eye, and like other wild beasts he quailed before the glance of mental and moral courage. He calmed down at once, and soon began to make apologies. Mr. B. then told him kindly, but firmly, that, if he wished to walk in the same path with him, he must walk as straight as the crack on the floor before them; adding that he would not walk with anybody who would jostle him by walking so crooked as he had done. He was perfectly tamed, and Mr. B. said he never had any more trouble with him."

The conviction here livingly enforced of the superiority on the side of the white man, was thus expressed by the Indian orator at Mackinaw while we were there. After the customary compliments about sun, dew, &c., "This," said he, "is the difference between the white and the red man; the white man looks to the future and paves the way for posterity." This is a statement uncommonly refined for an Indian; but one of the gentlemen present, who understood the Chippeway, vouched for it as a literal rendering of his phrases; and he did indeed touch the vital point of difference. But the Indian, if he understands, cannot make use of his intelligence. The fate of his people is against it, and Pontiac and Philip have no more chance, than Julian in the times of old.

Now that I am engaged on this subject, let me give some notices of writings upon it, read either at Mackinaw or since my return.

Mrs. Jameson made such good use of her brief visit to these regions, as leaves great cause to regret she did not stay longer and go farther; also, that she did not make more use of her acquaintance with, indeed, adoption by, the Johnson family. Mr. Johnson seems to have been almost the only white man who knew how to regard with due intelligence and nobleness, his connexion with the race. Neither French or English, of any powers of sympathy, or poetical apprehension, have lived among the Indians without high feelings of enjoyment. Perhaps no luxury has been greater, than that experienced by the persons, who, sent either by trade or war, during the last century, into these majestic regions, found guides and shelter amid the children of the soil, and recognized in a form so new and of such varied, yet simple, charms, the tie of brotherhood.

But these, even Sir William Johnston, whose life, surrounded by the Indians in his castle on the Mohawk, is described with such vivacity by Mrs. Grant, have been men better fitted to enjoy and adapt themselves to this life, than to observe and record it. The very faculties that made it so easy for them to live in the present moment, were likely to unfit them for keeping its chronicle. Men, whose life is full and instinctive, care little for the pen. But the father of Mrs. Schoolcraft seems to have taken pleasure in observation and comparison, and to have imparted the same tastes to his children. They have enough of European culture to have a standard, by which to judge their native habits and inherited lore.

By the premature death of Mrs. Schoolcraft was lost a mine of poesy, to which few had access, and from which Mrs. Jameson would have known how to coin a series of medals for the history of this ancient people. We might have known in clear outline, as now we shall not, the growths of religion and philosophy, under the influences of this climate and scenery, from such suggestions as nature and the teachings of the inward mind presented.

Now we can only gather that they had their own theory of the history of this globe; had perceived a gap in its genesis, and tried to fill it up by the intervention of some secondary power, with moral sympathies. They have observed the action of fire and water upon this earth; also that the dynasty of animals has yielded to that of man. With these animals they have profound sympathy, and are always trying to restore to them their lost honors. On the rattlesnake, the beaver, and the bear, they seem to look with a mixture of sympathy and veneration, as on their fellow settlers in these realms. There is something that appeals powerfully to the imagination in the ceremonies they observe, even in case of destroying one of these animals. I will say more of this by-and-by.

The dog they cherish as having been once a spirit of high intelligence; and now in its fallen, and imprisoned state, given to man as his special companion. He is therefore to them a sacrifice of peculiar worth: whether to a guardian spirit or a human friend. Yet nothing would be a greater violation than giving the remains of a sacrificial feast to the dogs, or even suffering them to touch the bones.

Similar inconsistences may be observed in the treatment of the dog by the white man. He is the most cherished companion in the familiar walks of many men; his virtues form the theme of poetry and history; the nobler races present grand traits, and are treated with proportionate respect. Yet the epithets dog and hound, are there set apart to express the uttermost contempt.

Goethe, who abhorred dogs, has selected that animal for the embodiment of the modern devil, who, in earlier times, chose rather the form of the serpent.

There is, indeed, something that peculiarly breaks in on the harmony of nature, in the bark of the dog, and that does not at all correspond with the softness and sagacity observable in his eye. The baying the moon, I have been inclined to set down as an unfavorable indication; but, since Fourier has found out that the moon is dead, and "no better than carrion;" and the Greeks have designated her as Hecate, the deity of suicide and witchcraft, the dogs are perhaps in the right.

They have among them the legend of the carbuncle, so famous in oriental mythos. Adair states that they believe this fabulous gem may be found on the spot where the rattlesnake has been destroyed.

If they have not the archetypal man, they have the archetypal animal, "the grandfather of all beavers;" to them, who do not know the elephant, this is the symbol of wisdom, as the rattlesnake and bear of power.

I will insert here a little tale about the bear, which has not before appeared in print, as representing their human way of looking on these animals, even when engaged in their pursuit. To me such stories give a fine sense of the lively perceptions and exercise of fancy, enjoyed by them in their lives of woodcraft:

MUCKWA, OR THE BEAR.

A young Indian, who lived a great while ago, when he was quite young killed a bear; and the tribe from that circumstance called him Muckwa. As he grew up he became an expert hunter, and his favorite game was the bear, many of which he killed. One day he started off to a river far remote from the lodges of his tribe, and where berries and grapes were very plenty, in pursuit of bears. He hunted all day but found nothing; and just at night he came to some lodges which he thought to be those of some of his tribe. He approached the largest of them, lifted the curtain at its entrance, and went in, when he perceived the inmates to be bears, who were seated around the fire smoking. He said nothing, but seated himself also and smoked the pipe which they offered him, in silence. An old grey bear, who was the chief, ordered supper to be brought for him, and after he had eaten it, addressed him as follows: "My son, I am glad to see you come among us in a friendly manner. You have been a great hunter, and all the she-bears of our tribe tremble when they hear your name. But cease to trouble us, and come and live with me; we have a very pleasant life, living upon the fruits of the earth; and in the winter, instead of being obliged to hunt and travel through the deep snow, we sleep soundly until the sun unchains the streams, and makes the tender buds put forth for our subsistence. I will give you my daughter for a wife, and we will live happily together." Muckwa was inclined to accept the old bear's offer; but when he saw the daughter, who came and took off his wet moccasons, and gave him dry ones, he thought that he had never seen any Indian woman so beautiful. He accepted the offer of the chief of the bears, and lived with his wife very happily for some time. He had by her two sons, one of whom was like an Indian, and the other like a bear. When the bear-child was oppressed with heat, his mother would take him into the deep cool caves, while the Indian-child would shiver with cold, and cry after her in vain. As the autumn advanced, the bears began to go out in search of acorns, and then the she-bear said to Muckwa, "Stay at home here and watch our house, while I go to gather some nuts." She departed and was gone for some days with her people. By-and-by Muckwa became tired of staying at home, and thought that he would go off to a distance and resume his favorite bear-hunting. He accordingly started off, and at last came to a grove of lofty oaks, which were full of large acorns. He found signs of bear, and soon espied a fat she-bear on the top of a tree. He shot at her with a good aim, and she fell, pierced by his unerring arrow. He went up to her, and found it was his sister-in-law, who reproached him with his cruelty, and told him to return to his own people. Muckwa returned quietly home, and pretended not to have left his lodge. However, the old chief understood, and was disposed to kill him in revenge; but his wife found means to avert her father's anger. The winter season now coming on, Muckwa prepared to accompany his wife into winter quarters; they selected a large tamarack tree, which was hollow, and lived there comfortably until a party of hunters discovered their retreat. The she-bear told Muckwa to remain quietly in the tree, and that she would decoy off the hunters. She came out of the hollow, jumped from a bough of the tree, and escaped unharmed, although the hunters shot after her. Some time after, she returned to the tree, and told Muckwa that he had better go back to his own people. "Since you have lived among us," said she, "we have nothing but ill-fortune; you have killed my sister; and now your friends have followed your footsteps to our retreats to kill us. The Indian and the bear cannot live in the same lodge, for the Master of Life has appointed for them different habitations." So Muckwa returned with his son to his own people; but he never after would shoot a she-bear, for fear that he should kill his wife."

I admire this story for the ***savoir faire***, the nonchalance, the Vivian Greyism of Indian life. It is also a poetical expression of the sorrows of unequal relations; those in which the Master of Life was not consulted. Is it not pathetic; the picture of the mother carrying off the child that was like herself into the deep, cool caves, while the other, shivering with cold, cried after her in vain? The moral, too, of Muckwa's return to the bear lodges, thinking to hide his sin by silence, while it was at once discerned by those connected with him, is fine.

We have a nursery tale, of which children never weary, of a little boy visiting a bear house and holding intercourse with them on terms as free as Muckwa did. So, perhaps, the child of Norman-Saxon blood, no less than the Indian, finds some pulse of the Orson in his veins.

As they loved to draw the lower forms of nature up to them, divining their histories, and imitating their ways, in their wild dances and paintings; even so did they love to look upward and people the atmosphere that enfolds the earth, with fairies and manitoes. The sister, obliged to leave her brother on the earth, bids him look up at evening, and he will see her painting her face in the west.

All places, distinguished in any way by nature, aroused the feelings of worship, which, however ignorant, are always elevating. See as instances in this kind, the stories of Nanabojou, and the Winnebago Prince, at the falls of St. Anthony.

As with the Greeks, beautiful legends grow up which express the aspects of various localities. From the distant sand-banks in the lakes, glittering in the sun, come stories of enchantresses combing, on the shore, the long golden hair of a beautiful daughter. The Lorelei of the Rhine, with her syren song, and the sad events that follow, is found on the lonely rocks of Lake Superior.

The story to which I now refer, may be found in a book called Life on the Lakes, or, a Trip to the Pictured Rocks. There are two which purport to be Indian tales; one is simply a romantic narrative, connected with a spot at Mackinaw, called

Robinson's Folly. This, no less than the other, was unknown to those persons I saw on the island; but as they seem entirely beyond the powers of the person who writes them down, and the other one has the profound and original meaning of Greek tragedy, I believe they must be genuine legends.

The one I admire is the story of a young warrior, who goes to keep, on these lonely rocks, the fast which is to secure him vision of his tutelary spirit. There the loneliness is broken by the voice of sweet music from the water. The Indian knows well that to break the fast, which is the crisis of his life, by turning his attention from seeking the Great Spirit, to any lower object, will deprive him through life of heavenly protection, probably call down the severest punishment.

But the temptation is too strong for him; like the victims of the Lorelei, he looks, like them beholds a maiden of unearthly beauty, to him the harbinger of earthly wo.

The development of his fate, that succeeds; of love, of heart-break, of terrible revenge, which back upon itself recoils, may vie with anything I have ever known of stern tragedy, is altogether unlike any other form, and with all the peculiar expression we see lurking in the Indian eye. The demon is not frightful and fantastic, like those that haunt the German forest; but terribly human, as if of full manhood, reared in the shadow of the black forests. An Indian sarcasm vibrates through it, which, with Indian fortitude, defies the inevitable torture.

The Indian is steady to that simple creed, which forms the basis of all this mythology; that there is a God, and a life beyond this; a right and wrong which each man can see, betwixt which each man should choose; that good brings with it its reward and vice its punishment. Their moral code, if not refined as that of civilized nations, is clear and noble in the stress laid upon truth and fidelity. And all unprejudiced observers bear testimony that the Indians, until broken from their old anchorage by intercourse with the whites, who offer them, instead, a religion of which they furnish neither interpretation nor example, were singularly virtuous, if virtue be allowed to consist in a man's acting up to his own ideas of right.

Old Adair, who lived forty years among the Indians; not these tribes, indeed, but the southern Indians; does great justice to their religious aspiration. He is persuaded that they are Jews, and his main object is to identify their manifold ritual, and customs connected with it, with that of the Jews. His narrative contains much that is worthless, and is written in the most tedious manner of the folios. But his devotion to the records of ancient Jewry, has really given him power to discern congenial traits elsewhere, and for the sake of what he has expressed of the noble side of Indian character, we pardon him our having to wade through so many imbecilities.

An infidel; he says, is, in their language, "one who has shaken hands with the accursed speech;" a religious man, "one who has shaken hands with the beloved speech." If this be a correct definition, we could wish Adair more religious.

He gives a fine account of their methods of purification. These show a deep reliance on the sustaining Spirit. By fasting and prayer they make ready for all important decisions and actions. Even for the war path, on which he is likely to endure such privations, the brave prepares by a solemn fast. His reliance is on the spirit in which he goes forth.

We may contrast with the opinion of the missionary, as given on a former page, the testimony of one, who knew them as Adair did, to their heroism under torture.

He gives several stories, illustrative both of their courage, fortitude, and resource in time of peril, of which I will cite only the two first.

"The Shawano Indians took a Muskohge warrior, known by the name of "Old Scrany;" they bastinadoed him in the usual manner, and condemned him to the fiery torture. He underwent a great deal, without showing any concern; his countenance and behavior were as if he suffered not the least pain, and was formed beyond the common laws of nature. He told them, with a bold voice, that he was a very noted warrior, and gained most of his martial preferments at the expense of their nation, and was desirous of showing them in the act of dying that he was still as much their superior, as when he headed his gallant countrymen against them. That, although he had fallen into their hands, in forfeiting the protection of the divine power, by some impurity or other, yet he had still so much virtue remaining, as would enable him to punish himself more exquisitely than all their despicable, ignorant crowd could possibly do, if they gave him liberty by untying him, and would hand to him one of the red hot gun-barrels out of the fire. The proposal, and his method of address, appeared so exceedingly bold and uncommon, that his request was granted. Then he suddenly seized one end of the red hot barrel, and, brandishing it from side to side, he found his way through the armed and surprised multitude, and leaped down a prodigious steep and high bank into a branch of the river, dived through it, ran over a small island, passed the other branch amidst a shower of bullets, and, though numbers of his eager enemies were in close pursuit of him, he got to a bramble swamp, and in that naked, mangled condition, reached his own country. He proved a sharp thorn in their side afterwards, to the day of his death.

The Shawano also captivated a warrior of the Anantooiah, and put him to the stake, according to their usual cruel solemnities. Having unconcernedly suffered much sharp torture, he told them with scorn, they did not know how to punish a noted enemy, therefore he was willing to teach them, and would confirm the truth of his assertion, if they allowed him the opportunity. Accordingly he requested of them a pipe and some tobacco, which was given him; as soon as he lighted it, he sat down, naked as he was, on the women's burning torches, that were within his circle, and continued smoking his pipe without the least discomposure. On this a head warrior leaped up, and said they had seen, plain enough, that he was a warrior, and not afraid of dying; nor should he have died, but that he was both spoiled by the fire, and devoted to it by their laws; however, though he was a very dangerous enemy, and his nation a treacherous people, it should appear they paid a regard to bravery, even in one, who was marked over the body with war streaks at the cost of many lives of their beloved kindred. And then, by way of favor, he, with his friendly tomahawk, put an end to all his pains: though this merciful but bloody instrument was ready some minutes before it gave the blow, yet, I was assured, the spectators could not perceive the sufferer to change, either his posture, or his steady, erect countenance in the least."

Some stories as fine, but longer, follow. In reference to which Adair says, "The intrepid behavior of these red stoics, their surprising contempt of and indifference to life or death, instead of lessening, helps to confirm our belief of that supernatural power, which supported the great number of primitive martyrs, who sealed the Christian faith with their blood. The Indians have as much belief and expectation of a future state, as the greater part of the Israelites seem to have. But the Christians of the first centuries, may justly be said to exceed even the most heroic American Indians, for they bore the bitterest persecution with steady patience, in imitation of their divine leader Messiah, in full confidence of divine support and of a glorious recompense of reward; and, instead of even wishing for revenge on their cruel enemies and malicious tormentors, (which is the chief principle that actuates the Indians,) they not only forgave them, but, in the midst of their tortures, earnestly prayed for them, with composed countenances, sincere love, and unabated fervor. And not only men of different conditions, but the delicate women and children suffered with constancy, and died praying for their tormentors: the Indian women and children, and their young men untrained to war, are incapable of displaying the like patience and magnanimity."

Thus impartially looks the old trader. I meant to have inserted other passages, that of the encampment at Yowanne, and the horse race to which he challenged them, to show how well he could convey in his garrulous fashion the whole presence of Indian life. That of Yowanne, especially, takes my fancy much, by its wild and subtle air, and the old-nurse fashion in which every look and gesture is detailed. His enjoyment, too, at outwitting the Indians in their own fashion is contagious. There is a fine history of a young man driven by a presentiment to run upon his death. But I find, to copy these stories, as they stand, would half fill this little book, and compression would spoil them, so I must wait some other occasion.

The story, later, of giving an Indian liquid fire to swallow, I give at full length, to show how a kind-hearted man and one well disposed towards them, can treat them, and view his barbarity as a joke. It is not then so much wonder, if the trader, with this same feeling that they may be treated, (as however brutes should not be,) brutally, mixes red pepper and damaged tobacco with the rum, intending in their fever to fleece them of all they possess.

Like Murray and Henry, he has his great Indian chief, who represents what the people should be, as Pericles and Phocion what the Greek people should be. If we are entitled to judge by its best fruits of the goodness of the tree, Adair's Red Shoes, and Henry's Wawatam, should make us respect the first possessors of our country, and doubt whether we are in all ways worthy to fill their place. Of the whole tone of character, judgment may be formed by what is said of the death of Red Shoes.

"This chief, by his several transcendent qualities had arrived at the highest pitch of the red glory....

He was murdered, for the sake of a French reward by one of his own countrymen. He had the misfortune to be taken very sick on the road, and to lodge apart from the camp, according to their custom. A Judas, tempted by the high reward of the French for killing him, officiously pretended to take great care of him. While Red Shoes kept his face toward him, the barbarian had such feelings of awe and pity that he had not power to perpetrate his wicked design; but when he turned his back, then gave the fatal shot. In this manner fell this valuable brave man, by hands that would have trembled to attack him on an equality."

Adair, with all his sympathy for the Indian, mixes quite unconsciously some white man's views of the most decided sort. For instance, he recommends that the tribes be stimulated as much as possible to war with each other, that they may the more easily and completely be kept under the dominion of the whites, and he gives the following record of brutality as quite a jocose and adroit procedure.

"I told him; on his importuning me further, that I had a full bottle of the water of **ane hoome**, "bitter ears," meaning long pepper, of which he was ignorant. We were of opinion that his eager thirst for liquor, as well as his ignorance of the burning quality of the pepper, would induce the bacchanal to try it. He accordingly applauded my generous disposition, and said his heart had all along told him I would not act beneath the character I bore among his country people. The bottle was brought, I laid it on the table, and then told him, as he was spitting very much, (a general custom among the Indians when they are eager for anything,) if I drank it all at one sitting it would cause me to spit in earnest, as I used it only when I ate, and then very moderately; but though I loved it, if his heart was very poor for it, I should be silent, and not the least grudge him for pleasing his mouth. He said, 'your heart is honest, indeed; I thank you, for it is good to my heart, and makes it greatly to rejoice.' Without any further ceremony he seized the bottle, uncorked it, and swallowed a large quantity of the burning liquid, till he was nearly strangled. He gasped for a considerable time, and as soon as he recovered his breath, he said **Hah**, and soon after kept stroking his throat with his right hand. When the violence of this burning draught was pretty well over, he began to flourish away in praise of the strength of the liquor and bounty of the giver. He then went to his companion and held the liquor to his mouth according to custom, till he took several hearty swallows. This Indian seemed rather more sensible of its fiery quality than the other, for it suffocated him for a considerable time; but as soon as he recovered his breath, he tumbled about the floor like a drunken person. In this manner they finished the whole bottle, into which two others had been decanted. The burning liquor so highly inflamed their bodies, that one of the Choctaws, to cool his inward parts, drank water till he almost burst; the other, rather than bear the ridicule of the people, and the inward fire that distracted him, drowned himself the second night after in a broad and shallow clay hole....

There was an incident similar, which happened among the Cherokees. When all the liquor was expended the Indians went home, leading with them, at my request, those that were drunk. One, however, soon came back, and earnestly importuned me for more Nawahti, which signifies both physic and spirituous liquor. They, as they are now become great liars, suspect all others of being infected with their own disposition and principles. The more I excused myself, the more anxious he grew, so as to become offensive. I then told him I had only one quarter of a bottle of strong physic, which sick people might drink in small quantities, for the cure of inward pains: and, laying it down before him, I declared I did not on any account choose to part with it, but as his speech had become very long and troublesome, he might do just as his heart directed him concerning it. He took it up, saying, his heart was very poor for physic, but he would cure it, and make it quite straight. The bottle contained three gills of strong spirits of turpentine, which, in a short time he drank off. Such a quantity would have demolished me or any white person. The Indians, in general, are either capable of suffering exquisite pain longer than we are, or of showing more constancy and composure in their torments. The troublesome visiter soon tumbled down and foamed prodigiously. I then sent for some of his relations to carry him home. They came; I told them he drank greedily, and too much of the physic. They said, it was his usual custom, when the red people bought the English physic. They gave him a decoction of proper herbs and roots, the next day sweated him, repeated the former draught, and he got well. As these turpentine spirits did not inebriate him, but only inflamed his intestines, he well remembered the burning quality of my favorite physic, and cautioned the rest from ever teasing me for any physic I had concealed in any sort of bottles for my own use; otherwise they might be sure it would spoil them like the eating of fire."

We are pleased to note that the same white man, who so resolutely resisted the encroachments of Key-way-no-wut, devised a more humane expedient in a similar dilemma.

"Mr. B. told me that, when he first went into the Indian country, they got the taste of his peppermint, and, after that, colics prevailed among them to an alarming extent, till Mrs. B. made a strong decoction of flagroot, and gave them in place of their favorite medicine. This effected, as might be supposed, a radical cure."

I am inclined to recommend Adair to the patient reader, if such may be found in these United States, with the assurance that, if he will have tolerance for its intolerable prolixity and dryness, he will find, on rising from the book, that he has partaken of an infusion of real Indian bitters, such as may not be drawn from any of the more attractive memoirs on the same subject.

Another book of interest, from its fidelity and candid spirit, though written without vivacity, and by a person neither of large mind nor prepared for various inquiry, is Carver's Travels, "for three years throughout the interior parts of America, for more than five thousand miles."

He set out from Boston in "June, 1786, and proceeded, by way of Albany and Niagara, to Michilimackinac, a fort situated between the Lakes Huron and Michigan, and distant from Boston 1300 miles."

It is interesting to follow his footsteps in these localities, though they be not bold footsteps.

He mentions the town of the Sacs, on the Wisconsin, as the largest and best built he saw, "composed of ninety houses, each large enough for several families. These are built of hewn plank, neatly jointed, and covered with bark so compactly as to keep out the most penetrating rains. Before the doors are placed comfortable sheds, in which the inhabitants sit, when the weather will permit, and smoke their pipes. The streets are regular and spacious. In their plantations, which lie adjacent to their houses, and which are neatly laid out, they raise great quantities of Indian corn, beans and melons."

Such settlements compare very well with those which were found on the Mohawk. It was of such that the poor Indian was thinking, whom our host saw gazing on the shore of Nomabbin lake.

He mentions the rise and fall of the lake-waters, by a tide of three feet, once in seven years,--a phenomenon not yet accounted for.

His view of the Indian character is truly impartial. He did not see it so fully drawn out by circumstances as Henry did, (of whose narrative we shall presently speak,) but we come to similar results from the two witnesses. They are in every feature Romans, as described by Carver, and patriotism their leading impulse. He deserves the more credit for the justice he is able to do them, that he had undergone the terrors of death at their hands, when present at the surrender of one of the forts, and had seen them in that mood which they express by drinking the blood and eating the hearts of their enemies, yet is able to understand the position of their minds, and allow for their notions of duty.

No selfish views, says he, influence their advice, or obstruct their consultations.

Let me mention here the use they make of their vapor baths. "When about to decide on some important measure, they go into them, thus cleansing the skin and carrying off any peccant humors, so that the body may, as little as possible, impede the mind by any ill conditions."

They prepare the bath for one another when any arrangement is to be made between families, on the opposite principle to the whites, who make them drunk before bargaining with them. The bath serves them instead of a cup of coffee, to stimulate the thinking powers.

He mentions other instances of their kind of delicacy, which, if different from ours, was, perhaps, more rigidly observed.

Lovers never spoke of love till the daylight was quite gone.

"If an Indian goes to visit any particular person in a family, he mentions for whom his visit is intended, and the rest of the family, immediately retiring to the other end of the hut or tent, are careful not to come near enough to interrupt them during the whole of the conversation."

In cases of divorce, which was easily obtained, the advantage rested with the woman. The reason given is indeed contemptuous toward her, but a chivalric direction is given to the contempt.

"The children of the Indians are always distinguished by the name of the mother, and, if a woman marries several husbands, and has issue by each of them, they are called after her. The reason they give for this is, that, 'as their offspring are indebted to the father for the soul, the invisible part of their essence, and to the mother for their corporeal and apparent part, it is most rational that they should be distinguished by the name of the latter, from whom they indubitably derive their present being.'"

This is precisely the division of functions made by Ovid, as the father sees Hercules perishing on the funeral pyre.

> "Nec nisi materna Vulcanum parte potentem
> Sentiet. Aeternum est a me quod traxit et expers
> Atque immune necis, nullaqe domabile flamma."

He is not enough acquainted with natural history to make valuable observations. He mentions, however, as did my friend, the Indian girl, that those splendid flowers, the Wickapee and the root of the Wake-Robin, afford valuable medicines. Here, as in the case of the Lobelia, nature has blazoned her drug in higher colors than did ever quack doctor.

He observes some points of resemblance between the Indians and Tartars, but they are trivial, and not well considered. He mentions that the Tartars have the same custom, with some of these tribes, of shaving all the head except a tuft on the crown. Catlin says this is intended, to afford a convenient means by which to take away the scalp; for they consider it a great disgrace to have the foeman neglect this, as if he considered the conquest, of which the scalp is the certificate, no addition to his honors.

"The Tartars," he says, "had a similar custom of sacrificing the dog; and among the Kamschatkans was a dance resembling the dog-dance of our Indians."

My friend, who joined me at Mackinaw, happened, on the homeward journey, to see a little Chinese girl, who had been sent over by one of the missions, and observed that, in features, complexion, and gesture, she was a counterpart to the little Indian girls she had just seen playing about on the lake shore.

The parentage of these tribes is still an interesting subject of speculation, though, if they be not created for this region, they have become so assimilated to it as to retain little trace of any other. To me it seems most probable, that a peculiar race was bestowed on each region, as the lion on one latitude and the white bear on another. As man has two natures--one, like that of the plants and animals, adapted to the uses and enjoyments of this planet, another, which presages and demands a higher sphere--he is constantly breaking bounds, in proportion as the mental gets the better of the mere instinctive existence. As yet, he loses in harmony of being what he gains in height and extension; the civilized man is a larger mind, but a more imperfect nature than the savage.

It is pleasant to meet, on the borders of these two states, one of those persons who combines some of the good qualities of both; not, as so many of these adventurers do, the rapaciousness and cunning of the white, with the narrowness and ferocity of the savage, but the sentiment and thoughtfulness of the one, with the boldness, personal resource, and fortitude of the other.

Such a person was Alexander Henry, who left Quebec in 1760, for Mackinaw and the Sault St. Marie, and remained in those regions, of which he has given us a most lively account, sixteen years.

His visit to Mackinaw was premature; the Indians were far from satisfied; they hated their new masters. From the first, the omens were threatening, and before many months passed, the discontent ended in the seizing of the fort at Mackinaw and massacre of its garrison; on which occasion Henry's life was saved by a fine act of Indian chivalry.

Wawatam, a distinguished chief, had found himself drawn, by strong affinity, to the English stranger. He had adopted him as a brother, in the Indian mode. When he found that his tribe had determined on the slaughter of the whites, he obtained permission to take Henry away with him, if he could. But not being able to prevail on him, as he could not assign the true reasons, he went away deeply saddened, but not without obtaining a promise that his brother should not be injured. The reason he was obliged to go, was, that his tribe felt his affections were so engaged, that his self-command could not be depended on to keep their secret. Their promise was not carefully observed, and, in consequence of the baseness of a French Canadian in whose house Henry took refuge,--baseness such as has not, even by their foes, been recorded of any Indian, his life was placed in great hazard. But Wawatam returned in time to save him. The scene in which he appears, accompanied by his wife--who seems to have gone hand in hand with him in this matter--lays down all his best things in a heap, in the middle of the hall, as a ransom for the captive, and his little, quiet speech, are as good as the Iliad. They have the same simplicity, the same lively force and tenderness.

Henry goes away with his adopted brother, and lives for some time among the tribe. The details of this life are truly interesting. One time he is lost for several days while on the chase. The description of these weary, groping days, the aspect of natural objects and of the feelings thus inspired, and the mental change after a good night's sleep, form a little episode worthy the epic muse. He stripped off the entire bark of a tree for a coverlet in the snow-storm, going to sleep with "the most distracted thoughts in the world, while the wolves around seemed to know the distress to which he was reduced;" but he waked in the morning another man, clear-headed, able to think out the way to safety.

When living in the lodge, he says: "At one time much scarcity of food prevailed. We were often twenty-four hours without eating; and when in the morning we had no victuals for the day before us, the custom was to black our faces with grease and charcoal, and exhibit, through resignation, a temper as cheerful as in the midst of plenty." This wise and dignified proceeding reminds one of a charming expression of what is best in French character, as described by Rigolette, in the Mysteries of Paris, of the household of Pere Cretu and Ramnonette.

He bears witness to much virtue among them. Their superstitions, as described by him, seem childlike and touching. He gives with much humor, traits that show their sympathy with the lower animals, such as I have mentioned. He speaks of them as, on the whole, taciturn, because their range of topics is so limited, and seems to have seen nothing of their talent for narration. Catlin, on the contrary, describes them as lively and garrulous, and says, that their apparent taciturnity among the whites is owing to their being surprised at what they see, and unwilling, from pride, to show that they are so, as well as that they have little to communicate on their side, that they think will be valuable.

After peace was restored, and Henry lived long at Mackinaw and the Sault St. Marie, as a trader, the traits of his biography and intercourse with the Indians, are told in the same bold and lively style. I wish I had room for many extracts, as the book is rare.

He made a journey one winter on snow shoes, to Prairie du Chien, which is of romantic interest as displaying his character. His companions could not travel nearly so fast as he did, and detained him on the way. Provisions fell short; soon they were ready to perish of starvation. Apprehending this, on a long journey, in the depth of winter, broken by no hospitable station, Henry had secreted some chocolate. When he saw his companions ready to lie down and die, he would heat water, boil in it a square of this, and give them. By the heat of the water and the fancy of nourishment, they would be revived, and induced to proceed a little further. At last they saw antlers sticking up from the ice, and found the body of an elk, which had sunk in and been frozen there, and thus preserved to save their lives. On this "and excellent soup" made from bones they found they were sustained to their journey's end; thus furnishing, says Henry, one other confirmation of the truth, that "despair was not made for man;" this expression, and his calm consideration for the Canadian women that was willing to betray him to death, denote the two sides of a fine character.

He gives an interesting account of the tribe called "The Weepers," on account of the rites with which they interrupt their feasts in honor of their friends.

He gives this humorous notice of a chief, called "The Great Road."

"The chief, to whose kindly reception we were so much indebted, was of a complexion rather darker than that of the Indians in general. His appearance was greatly injured by the condition of his hair, and this was the result of an extraordinary superstition.

"The Indians universally fix upon a particular object as sacred to themselves--as the giver of prosperity and as their preserver from evil. The choice is determined either by a dream or some strong predilection of fancy, and usually falls upon an animal, part of an animal, or something else which is to be met with by land, or by water; but the Great Road had made choice of his hair, placing, like Samson, all his safety in this portion of his proper substance! His hair was the fountain of all his happiness; it was his strength and his weapon--his spear and his shield. It preserved him in battle, directed him in the chase, watched over him in the march, and gave length of days to his wives and children. Hair, of a quality like this, was not to be profaned by the touch of human hands. I was assured that it never had been cut nor combed from his childhood upward, and that when any part of it fell from his head, he treasured that part with, care; meanwhile, it did not escape all care, even while growing on the head, but was in the especial charge of a spirit, who dressed it while the owner slept. The spirit's style of hair-dressing was peculiar, the hair being matted into ropes, which spread in all directions."

I insert the following account of a visit from some Indians to him at Mackinaw, with a design to frighten him, and one to Carver, for the same purpose, as very descriptive of Indian manners:

"At two o'clock in the afternoon, the Chippeways came to my house, about sixty in number, and headed by Mina-va-va-na, their chief. They walked in single file, each with his tomahawk in one hand, and scalping knife in the other. Their bodies were naked, from the waist upwards, except in a few examples, where blankets were thrown loosely over the shoulders. Their faces were painted with charcoal, worked up with grease; their bodies with white clay in patterns of various fancies. Some had feathers thrust through their noses, and their heads decorated with the same. It is unnecessary to dwell on the sensations with which I beheld the approach of this uncouth, if not frightful, assemblage."

"Looking out, I saw about twenty naked young Indians, the most perfect in their shape, and by far the handsomest I had ever seen, coming towards me, and dancing as they approached to the music of their drums. At every ten or twelve yards they halted, and set up their yells and cries.

When they reached my tent I asked them to come in, which, without deigning to make me any answer, they did. As I observed they were painted red and black, as they are when they go against an enemy, and perceived that some parts of the war-dance were intermixed with their other movements, I doubted not but they were set on by the hostile chief who refused my salutation. I therefore determined to sell my life as dearly as possible. To this purpose I received them sitting on my chest, with my gun and pistols beside me; and ordered my men to keep a watchful eye on them, and be also on their guard.

The Indians being entered, they continued their dance alternately, singing at the same time of their heroic exploits, and the superiority of their race over every other people. To enforce their language, though it was uncommonly nervous and expressive, and such as would of itself have carried terror to the firmest heart; at the end of every period they struck their war-clubs against the poles of my tent with such violence, that I expected every moment it would have tumbled upon us. As each of them in dancing round passed by me, they placed their right hands over their eyes, and coming close to me, looked me steadily in the face, which I could not construe into a token of friendship. My men gave themselves up for lost; and I acknowledge for my own part, that I never found my apprehensions more tumultuous on any occasion."

He mollified them, however, in the end by presents.

It is pity that Lord Edward Fitzgerald did not leave a detailed account of his journey through the wilderness, where he was pilot of an unknown course for twenty days, as Murray and Henry have of theirs. There is nothing more interesting than to see the civilized man thus thrown wholly on himself and his manhood, and ***not*** found at fault.

McKenney and Hall's book upon the Indians is a valuable work. The portraits of the chiefs alone would make a history, and they are beautifully colored.

Most of the anecdotes may be found again in Drake's Book of the Indians; which will afford a useful magazine to their future historian.

I shall, however, cite a few of them, as especially interesting to myself.

Of Guess, the inventor of the Cherokee alphabet, it was observable in the picture, and observed in the text, that his face had an oriental cast. The same, we may recall, was said of that of the Seeress of Prevorst, and the circumstance presents pleasing analogies. Intellect dawning through features still simple and national, presents very different apparitions from the "expressive" and "historical" faces of a broken and cultured race, where there is always more to divine than to see.

Of the picture of the Flying Pigeon, the beautiful and excellent woman mentioned above, a keen observer said, "If you cover the forehead, you would think the face that of a Madonna, but the forehead is still savage; the perceptive faculties look so sharp, and the forehead not moulded like a European forehead." This is very true; in her the moral nature was most developed, and the effect of a higher growth upon her face is entirely different from that upon Guess.

His eye is inturned, while the proper Indian eye gazes steadily, as if on a distant object. That is half the romance of it, that it makes you think of dark and distant places in the forest.

Guess always preferred inventing his implements to receiving them from others: and, when considered as mad by his tribe, while bent on the invention of his alphabet, contented himself with teaching it to his little daughter; an unimpeachable witness.

Red Jacket's face, too, is much more intellectual than almost any other. But, in becoming so, it loses nothing of the peculiar Indian stamp, but only carries these traits to their perfection. Irony, discernment, resolution, and a deep smouldering fire, that disdains to flicker where it cannot blaze, may there be read. Nothing can better represent the sort of unfeelingness the whites have towards the Indians, than their conduct towards his remains. He had steadily opposed the introduction of white religion, or manners, among the Indians. He believed that for them to break down the barriers was to perish. On many occasions he had expressed this with all the force of his eloquence. He told the preachers, "if the Great Spirit had meant your religion for the red man, he would have given it to them. What they (the missionaries) tell us, we do not understand; and the light they ask for us, makes the straight and plain path trod by our fathers dark and dreary."

When he died, he charged his people to inter him themselves. "Dig my grave, yourselves, and let not the white man pursue me there." In defiance of this last solemn request, and the invariable tenor of his life, the missionaries seized the body and performed their service over it, amid the sullen indignation of his people, at what, under the circumstances, was sacrilege.

Of Indian religion a fine specimen is given in the conduct of one of the war chiefs, who, on an important occasion, made a vow to the sun of entire renunciation in case he should be crowned with success. When he was so, he first went through a fast, and sacrificial dance, involving great personal torment, and lasting several days; then, distributing all his property, even his lodges, and mats, among the tribe, he and his family took up their lodging upon the bare ground, beneath the bare sky.

The devotion of the Stylites and the hair-cloth saints, is in act, though not in motive, less noble, because this great chief proposed to go on in common life, where he had lived as a prince--a beggar.

The memoir by Corn Plant of his early days is beautiful.

Very fine anecdotes are told of two of the Western chiefs, father and son, who had the wisdom to see the true policy toward the whites, and steadily to adhere to it.

A murder having taken place in the jurisdiction of the father, he delivered himself up, with those suspected, to imprisonment. One of his companions chafed bitterly under confinement. He told the chief, if they ever got out, he would kill him, and did so. The son, then a boy, came in his rage and sorrow, to this Indian, and insulted him in every way. The squaw, angry at this, urged her husband "to kill the boy at once." But he only replied with "the joy of the valiant," "He will be a great Brave," and then delivered himself up to atone for his victim, and met his death with the noblest Roman composure.

This boy became rather a great chief than a great brave, and the anecdotes about him are of signal beauty and significance.

There is a fine story of an old mother, who gave herself to death instead of her son. The son, at the time, accepted the sacrifice, seeing, with Indian coolness, that it was better she should give up her few solitary and useless days, than he a young existence full of promise. But he could not abide by this view, and after suffering awhile all the anguish of remorse, he put himself solemnly to death in the presence of the tribe, as the only atonement he could make. His young wife stood by, with her child in her arms, commanding her emotions, as he desired, for, no doubt, it seemed to her also, a sacred duty.

But the finest story of all is that of Petalesharro, in whose tribe at the time, and not many years since, the custom of offering human sacrifices still subsisted. The fire was kindled, the victim, a young female captive, bound to the stake, the tribe assembled round. The young brave darted through them, snatched the girl from her peril, placed her upon his horse, and both had vanished before the astonished spectators had thought to interpose.

He placed the girl in her distant home, and then returned. Such is the might of right, when joined with courage, that none ventured a word of resentment or question. His father, struck by truth, endeavored, and with success, to abolish the barbarous custom in the tribe. On a later occasion, Petalesharro again offered his life, if required, but it was not.

This young warrior visiting Washington, a medal was presented him in honor of these acts. His reply deserves sculpture: "When I did it, I knew not that it was good. I did it in ignorance. This medal makes me know that it was good."

The recorder, through his playful expressions of horror at a declaration so surprising to the civilized Good, shows himself sensible to the grand simplicity of heroic impulse it denotes. Were we, too, so good, as to need a medal to show us that we are!

The half-breed and half-civilized chiefs, however handsome, look vulgar beside the pure blood. They have the dignity of neither race.

The death of Oseola, (as described by Catlin,) presents a fine picture in the stern, warlike kind, taking leave with kindness, as a private friend, of the American officers; but, as a foe in national regards, he raised himself in his dying bed, and painted his face with the tokens of eternal enmity.

The historian of the Indians should be one of their own race, as able to sympathize with them, and possessing a mind as enlarged and cultivated as John Ross, and with his eye turned to the greatness of the past, rather than the scanty promise of the future. Hearing of the wampum belts, supposed to have been sent to our tribes by Montezuma, on the invasion of the Spaniard, we feel that an Indian who could glean traditions familiarly from the old men, might collect much that we could interpret.

Still, any clear outline, even of a portion of their past, is not to be hoped, and we shall be well contented if we can have a collection of genuine fragments, that will indicate as clearly their life, as a horse's head from the Parthenon the genius of Greece.

Such, to me, are the stories I have cited above. And even European sketches of this greatness, distant and imperfect though they be, yet convey the truth, if made in a sympathizing spirit. Adair's Red Shoes, Murray's old man, Catlin's noble Mandan chief, Henry's Wa-wa-tam, with what we know of Philip, Pontiac, Tecumseh and Red Jacket, would suffice to give the ages a glimpse at what was great in Indian life and Indian character.

We hope, too, there will be a national institute, containing all the remains of the Indians,--all that has been preserved by official intercourse at Washington, Catlin's collection, and a picture gallery as complete as can be made, with a collection of skulls from all parts of the country. To this should be joined the scanty library that exists on the subject.

I have not mentioned Mackenzie's Travels. He is an accurate observer, but sparing in his records, because his attention was wholly bent on his own objects. This circumstance gives a heroic charm to his scanty and simple narrative. Let what will happen, or who will go back, he cannot; he must find the sea, along those frozen rivers, through those starving countries, among tribes of stinted men, whose habitual interjection was "edui, it is hard, uttered in a querulous tone," distrusted by his followers, deserted by his guides, on, on he goes, till he sees the sea, cold, lowering, its strand bristling with foes; but he does see it.

His few observations, especially on the tribes who lived on fish, and held them in such superstitious observance, give a lively notion of the scene.

A little pamphlet has lately been published, giving an account of the massacre at Chicago, which I wish much I had seen while there, as it would have imparted an interest to spots otherwise barren. It is written with animation, and in an excellent style, telling just what we want to hear, and no more. The traits given of Indian generosity are as characteristic as those of Indian cruelty. A lady, who was saved by a friendly chief holding her under the waters of the lake, while the balls were whizzing around, received also, in the heat of the conflict, a reviving draught from a squaw, who saw she was exhausted; and, as she lay down, a mat was hung up between her and the scene of butchery, so that she was protected from the sight, though she could not be from sounds, full of horror.

I have not wished to write sentimentally about the Indians, however moved by the thought of their wrongs and speedy extinction. I know that the Europeans who took possession of this country, felt themselves justified by their superior civilization and religious ideas. Had they been truly civilized or Christianized, the conflicts which sprang from the collision of the two races, might have been avoided; but this cannot be expected in movements made by masses of men. The mass has never yet been humanized, though the age may develop a human thought.

Since those conflicts and differences did arise, the hatred which sprang, from terror and suffering, on the European side, has naturally warped the whites still farther from justice.

The Indian, brandishing the scalps of his friends and wife, drinking their blood and eating their hearts, is by him viewed as a fiend, though, at a distant day, he will no doubt be considered as having acted the Roman or Carthaginian part of heroic and patriotic self-defence, according to the standard of right and motives prescribed by his religious faith and education. Looked at by his own standard, he is virtuous when he most injures his enemy, and the white, if he be really the superior in enlargement of thought, ought to cast aside his inherited prejudices enough to see this,--to look on him in pity and brotherly goodwill, and do all he can to mitigate the doom of those who survive his past injuries.

In McKenney's book, is proposed a project for organizing the Indians under a patriarchal government, but it does not look feasible, even on paper. Could their own intelligent men be left to act unimpeded in their behalf, they would do far better for them than the white thinker, with all his general knowledge. But we dare not hope the designs of such will not always be frustrated by the same barbarous selfishness they were in Georgia. There was a chance of seeing what might have been done, now lost forever.

Yet let every man look to himself how far this blood shall be required at his hands. Let the missionary, instead of preaching to the Indian, preach to the trader who ruins him, of the dreadful account which will be demanded of the followers of Cain, in a sphere where the accents of purity and love come on the ear more decisively than in ours. Let every legislator take the subject to heart, and if he cannot undo the effects of past sin, try for that clear view and right sense that may save us from sinning still more deeply. And let every man and every woman, in their private dealings with the subjugated race, avoid all share in embittering, by insult or unfeeling prejudice, the captivity of Israel.

CHAPTER VII.
SAULT ST. MARIE.

Nine days I passed alone at Mackinaw, except for occasional visits from kind and agreeable residents at the fort, and Mr. and Mrs. A. Mr. A., long engaged in the fur-trade, is gratefully remembered by many travellers. From Mrs. A., also, I received kind attentions, paid in the vivacious and graceful manner of her nation.

The society at the boarding house entertained, being of a kind entirely new to me. There were many traders from the remote stations, such as La Pointe, Arbre Croche,--men who had become half wild and wholly rude, by living in the wild; but good-humored, observing, and with a store of knowledge to impart, of the kind proper to their place.

There were two little girls here, that were pleasant companions for me. One gay, frank, impetuous, but sweet and winning. She was an American, fair, and with bright brown hair. The other, a little French Canadian, used to join me in my walks, silently take my hand, and sit at my feet when I stopped in beautiful places. She seemed to understand without a word; and I never shall forget her little figure, with its light, but pensive motion, and her delicate, grave features, with the pale, clear complexion and soft eye. She was motherless, and much left alone by her father and brothers, who were boatmen. The two little girls were as pretty representatives of Allegro and Penseroso, as one would wish to see.

I had been wishing that a boat would come in to take me to the Sault St. Marie, and several times started to the window at night in hopes that the pant and dusky-red light crossing the waters belonged to such an one; but they were always boats for Chicago or Buffalo, till, on the 28th of August, Allegro, who shared my plans and wishes, rushed in to tell me that the General Scott had come, and, in this little steamer, accordingly, I set off the next morning.

I was the only lady, and attended in the cabin by a Dutch girl and an Indian woman. They both spoke English fluently, and entertained me much by accounts of their different experiences.

The Dutch girl told me of a dance among the common people at Amsterdam, called the shepherd's dance. The two leaders are dressed as shepherd and shepherdess; they invent to the music all kinds of movements, descriptive of things that may happen in the field, and the rest were obliged to follow. I have never heard of any dance which gave such free play to the fancy as this. French dances merely describe the polite movements of society; Spanish and Neapolitan, love; the beautiful Mazurkas, &c., are warlike or expressive of wild scenery. But in this one is great room both for fun and fancy.

The Indian was married, when young, by her parents, to a man she did not love. He became dissipated, and did not maintain her. She left him. taking with her their child; for whom and herself she earns a subsistence by going as chambermaid in these boats. Now and then, she said, her husband called on her, and asked if he might live with her again; but she always answered, no. Here she was far freer than she would have been in civilized life.

I was pleased by the nonchalance of this woman, and the perfectly national manner she had preserved after so many years of contact with all kinds of people. The two women, when I left the boat, made me presents of Indian work, such as travellers value, and the manner of the two was characteristic of their different nations. The Indian brought me hers, when I was alone, looked bashfully down when she gave it, and made an almost sentimental little speech. The Dutch girl brought hers in public, and, bridling her short chin with a self-complacent air, observed she had ***bought*** it for me. But the feeling of affectionate regard was the same in the minds of both.

Island after island we passed, all fairly shaped and clustering friendly, but with little variety of vegetation.

In the afternoon the weather became foggy, and we could not proceed after dark. That was as dull an evening as ever fell.

The next morning the fog still lay heavy, but the captain took me out in his boat on an exploring expedition, and we found the remains of the old English fort on Point St. Joseph's. All around was so wholly unmarked by anything but stress of wind and weather, the shores of these islands and their woods so like one another, wild and lonely, but nowhere rich and majestic, that there was some charm in the remains of the garden, the remains even of chimneys and a pier. They gave feature to the scene.

Here I gathered many flowers, but they were the same as at Mackinaw.

The captain, though he had been on this trip hundreds of times, had never seen this spot, and never would, but for this fog, and his desire to entertain me. He presented a striking instance how men, for the sake of getting a living, forget to live. It is just the same in the most romantic as the most dull and vulgar places. Men get the harness on so fast, that they can never shake it off unless they guard against this danger from the very first. In Chicago, how many men, who never found time to see the prairies or learn anything unconnected with the business of the day, or about the country they were living in!

So this captain, a man of strong sense and good eyesight, rarely found time to go off the track or look about him on it. He lamented, too, that there had been no call which induced him to develop his powers of expression, so that he might communicate what he had seen, for the enjoyment or instruction of others.

This is a common fault among the active men, the truly living, who could tell what life is. It should not be so. Literature should not be left to the mere literati--eloquence to the mere orator. Every Caesar should be able to write his own commentary. We want a more equal, more thorough, more harmonious development, and there is nothing to hinder from it the men of this country, except their own supineness, or sordid views.

When the weather did clear, our course up the river was delightful. Long stretched before us the island of St. Joseph's, with its fair woods of sugar maple. A gentleman on board, who belongs to the Fort at the Sault, said their pastime was to come in the season of making sugar, and pass some time on this island,--the days at work, and the evening in dancing and other amusements.

I wished to extract here Henry's account of this, for it was just the same sixty years ago as now, but have already occupied too much room with extracts. Work of this kind done in the open air, where everything is temporary, and every utensil prepared on the spot, gives life a truly festive air. At such times, there is labor and no care--energy with gaiety, gaiety of the heart.

I think with the same pleasure of the Italian vintage, the Scotch harvest-home, with its evening dance in the barn, the Russian cabbage-feast even, and our huskings and hop-gatherings--the hop-gatherings where the groups of men and girls are pulling down and filling baskets with the gay festoons, present as graceful pictures as the Italian vintage.

I should also like to insert Henry's descriptions of the method of catching trout and white fish, the delicacies of this region, for the same reason as I want his account of the Gens de Terre, the savages among savages, and his tales, dramatic, if not true, of cannibalism.

I have no less grieved to omit Carver's account of the devotion of a Winnebago prince at the Falls of St. Anthony, which he describes with a simplicity and intelligence, that are very pleasing.

I take the more pleasure in both Carver and Henry's power of appreciating what is good in the Indian character, that both had run the greatest risk of losing their lives during their intercourse with the Indians, and had seen them in their utmost exasperation, with all its revolting circumstances.

I wish I had a thread long enough to string on it all these beads that take my fancy; but, as I have not, I can only refer the reader to the books themselves, which may be found in the library of Harvard College, if not elsewhere.

How pleasant is the course along a new river, the sight of new shores; like a life, would but life flow as fast, and upbear us with as full a stream. I hoped we should come in sight of the rapids by daylight; but the beautiful sunset was quite gone, and only a young moon trembling over the scene, when we came within hearing of them.

I sat up long to hear them merely. It was a thoughtful hour. These two days, the 29th and 30th August, are memorable in my life; the latter is the birthday of a near friend. I pass them alone, approaching Lake Superior; but I shall not enter into that truly wild and free region; shall not have the canoe voyage, whose daily adventure, with the camping out at night beneath the stars, would have given an interlude of such value to my existence. I shall not see the Pictured Rocks, their chapels and urns. It did not depend on me; it never has, whether such things shall be done or not.

My friends! may they see, and do, and be more, especially those who have before them a greater number of birthdays, and of a more healthy and unfettered existence:

TO EDITH, ON HER BIRTHDAY.

If the same star our fates together bind,
Why are we thus divided, mind from mind?
If the same law one grief to both impart,
How could'st thou grieve a trusting mother's heart?

Our aspiration seeks a common aim,
Why were we tempered of such differing frame?
--But 'tis too late to turn this wrong to right;
Too cold, too damp, too deep, has fallen the night.

And yet, the angel of my life replies,
Upon that night a Morning Star shall rise,
Fairer than that which ruled the temporal birth,
Undimmed by vapors of the dreamy earth;

It says, that, where a heart thy claim denies,
Genius shall read its secret ere it flies;
The earthly form may vanish from thy side,
Pure love will make thee still the spirit's bride.

And thou, ungentle, yet much loving child,
Whose heart still shows the "untamed haggard wild,"
A heart which justly makes the highest claim,
Too easily is checked by transient blame;

Ere such an orb can ascertain its sphere,
The ordeal must be various and severe;

My prayers attend thee, though the feet may fly,
I hear thy music in the silent, sky.

I should I should like, however, to hear some notes of earthly music to-night. By the faint moonshine I can hardly see the banks; how they look I have no guess, except that there are trees, and, now and then, a light lets me know there are homes with their various interests. I should like to hear some strains of the flute from beneath those trees, just to break the sound of the rapids.

When no gentle eyebeam charms;
No fond hope the bosom warms:
Of thinking the lone mind is tired--
Nought seems bright to be desired;

Music, be thy sails unfurled,
Bear me to thy better world;
O'er a cold and weltering sea,
Blow thy breezes warm and free;

By sad sighs they ne'er were chilled,
By sceptic spell were never stilled;
Take me to that far-offshore,
Where lovers meet to part no more;
 There doubt, and fear and sin are o'er,
 The star of love shall set no more.

With the first light of dawn I was up and out, and then was glad I had not seen all the night before; it came upon me with such power in its dewy freshness. O! they are beautiful indeed, these rapids! The grace is so much more obvious than the power. I went up through the old Chippeway burying ground to their head, and sat down on a large stone to look. A little way off was one of the home lodges, unlike in shape to the temporary ones at Mackinaw, but these have been described by Mrs. Jameson. Women, too, I saw coming home from the woods, stooping under great loads of cedar boughs, that were strapped upon their backs. But in many European countries women carry great loads, even of wood, upon their backs. I used to hear the girls singing and laughing as they were cutting down boughs at Mackinaw; this part of their employment, though laborious, gives them the pleasure of being a great deal in the free woods.

I had ordered a canoe to take me down the rapids, and presently I saw it coming, with the two Indian canoe-men in pink calico shirts, moving it about with their long poles, with a grace and dexterity worthy fairy land. Now and then they cast the scoop-net; all looked just as I had fancied, only far prettier.

When they came to me, they spread a mat in the middle of the canoe; I sat down, and in less than four minutes we had descended the rapids, a distance of more than three quarters of a mile. I was somewhat disappointed in this being no more of an exploit than I found it. Having heard such expressions used as of "darting," or, "shooting down," these rapids, I had fancied there was a wall of rock somewhere, where descent would somehow be accomplished, and that there would come some one gasp of terror and delight, some sensation entirely new to me; but I found myself in smooth water, before I had time to feel anything but the buoyant pleasure of being carried so lightly through this surf amid the breakers. Now and then the Indians spoke to one another in a vehement jabber, which, however, had no tone that expressed other than pleasant excitement. It is, no doubt, an act of wonderful dexterity to steer amid these jagged rocks, when one rude touch would tear a hole in the birch canoe; but these men are evidently so used to doing it, and so adroit, that the silliest person could not feel afraid. I should like to have come down twenty times, that I might have had leisure to realize the pleasure. But the fog which had detained us on the way, shortened the boat's stay at the Sault, and I wanted my time to walk about.

While coming down the rapids, the Indians caught a white-fish for my breakfast; and certainly it was the best of breakfasts. The white-fish I found quite another thing caught on this spot, and cooked immediately, from what I had found it at Chicago or Mackinaw. Before, I had had the bad taste to prefer the trout, despite the solemn and eloquent remonstrances of the Habitues, to whom the superiority of white fish seemed a cardinal point of faith.

I am here reminded that I have omitted that indispensable part of a travelling journal, the account of what we found to eat. I cannot hope to make up, by one bold stroke, all my omissions of daily record; but that I may show myself not destitute of the common feelings of humanity, I will observe that he whose affections turn in summer towards vegetables, should not come to this region, till the subject of diet be better understood; that of fruit, too, there is little yet, even at the best hotel tables; that the prairie chickens require no praise from me, and that the trout and white-fish are worthy the transparency of the lake waters.

In this brief mention I by no means mean to give myself an air of superiority to the subject. If a dinner in the Illinois woods, on dry bread and drier meat, with water from the stream that flowed hard by, pleased me best of all, yet at one time, when living at a house where nothing was prepared for the table fit to touch, and even the bread could not be partaken of without a headach in consequence, I learnt to understand and sympathize with the anxious tone in which fathers of families, about to take their innocent children into some scene of wild beauty, ask first of all, "Is there a good table?" I shall ask just so in future. Only those whom the Powers have furnished small travelling cases of ambrosia, can take exercise all day, and be happy without even bread morning or night.

Our voyage back was all pleasure. It was the fairest day. I saw the river, the islands, the clouds to the greatest advantage.

On board was an old man, an Illinois farmer, whom I found a most agreeable companion. He had just been with his son, and eleven other young men, on an exploring expedition to the shores of lake Superior. He was the only old man of the party, but he had enjoyed, most of any, the journey. He had been the counsellor and playmate, too, of the young ones. He was one of those parents,--why so rare?--who understand and live a new life in that of their children, instead of wasting time and young happiness in trying to make them conform to an object and standard of their own. The character and history of each child may be a new and poetic experience to the parent, if he will let it. Our farmer was domestic, judicious, solid; the son, inventive, enterprising, superficial, full of follies, full of resources, always liable to failure, sure to rise above it. The father conformed to, and learnt from, a character he could not change, and won the sweet from the bitter.

His account of his life at home, and of his late adventures among the Indians, was very amusing, but I want talent to write it down. I have not heard the slang of these people intimately enough. There is a good book about Indiana, called the New Purchase, written by a person who knows the people of the country well enough to describe them in their own way. It is not witty, but penetrating, valuable for its practical wisdom and good-humored fun.

There were many sportsman stories told, too, by those from Illinois and Wisconsin. I do not retain any of these well enough, nor any that I heard earlier, to write them down, though they always interested me from bringing wild, natural scenes before the mind. It is pleasant for the sportsman to be in countries so alive with game; yet it is so plenty that one would think shooting pigeons or grouse would seem more like slaughter, than the excitement of skill to a good sportsman. Hunting the deer is full of adventure, and needs only a Scrope to describe it to invest the western woods with ***historic*** associations.

How pleasant it was to sit and hear rough men tell pieces out of their own common lives, in place of the frippery talk of some fine circle with its conventional sentiment, and timid, second-hand criticism. Free blew the wind, and boldly flowed the stream, named for Mary mother mild.

A fine thunder shower came on in the afternoon. It cleared at sunset, just as we came in sight of beautiful Mackinaw, over which a rainbow bent in promise of peace.

I have always wondered, in reading travels, at the childish joy travellers felt at meeting people they knew, and their sense of loneliness when they did not, in places where there was everything new to occupy the attention. So childish, I thought, always to be longing for the new in the old, and the old in the new. Yet just such sadness I felt, when I looked on the island, glittering in the sunset, canopied by the rainbow, and thought no friend would welcome me there; just such childish joy I felt, to see unexpectedly on the landing, the face of one whom I called friend.

The remaining two or three days were delightfully spent, in walking or boating, or sitting at the window to see the Indians go. This was not quite so pleasant as their coming in, though accomplished with the same rapidity; a family not taking half an hour to prepare for departure, and the departing canoe a beautiful object. But they left behind, on all the shore, the blemishes of their stay--old rags, dried boughs, fragments of food, the marks of their fires. Nature likes to cover up and gloss over spots and scars, but it would take her some time to restore that beach to the state it was in before they came.

S. and I had a mind for a canoe excursion, and we asked one of the traders to engage us two good Indians, that would not only take us out, but be sure and bring us back, as we could not hold converse with them. Two others offered their aid, beside the chief's son, a fine looking youth of about sixteen, richly dressed in blue broadcloth, scarlet sash and leggins, with a scarf of brighter red than the rest, tied around his head, its ends falling gracefully on one shoulder. They thought it, apparently, fine amusement to be attending two white women; they carried us into the path of the steamboat, which was going out, and paddled with all their force,--rather too fast, indeed, for there was something of a swell on the lake, and they sometimes threw water into the canoe. However, it flew over the waves, light as a sea-gull. They would say, "Pull away," and "Ver' warm," and, after these words, would laugh gaily. They enjoyed the hour, I believe, as much as we.

The house where we lived belonged to the widow of a French trader, an Indian by birth, and wearing the dress of her country. She spoke French fluently, and was very ladylike in her manners. She is a great character among them. They were all the time coming to pay her homage, or to get her aid and advice; for she is, I am told, a shrewd woman of business. My companion carried about her sketch-book with her, and the Indians were interested when they saw her using her pencil, though less so than about the sun-shade. This lady of the tribe wanted to borrow the sketches of the beach, with its lodges and wild groups, "to show to the ***savages***," she said.

Of the practical ability of the Indian women, a good specimen is given by McKenney, in an amusing story of one who went to Washington, and acted her part there in the "first circles," with a tact and sustained dissimulation worthy of Cagliostro. She seemed to have a thorough love of intrigue for its own sake, and much dramatic talent. Like the chiefs of her nation, when on an expedition among the foe, whether for revenge or profit, no impulses of vanity or wayside seductions had power to turn her aside from carrying out her plan as she had originally projected it.

Although I have little to tell, I feel that I have learnt a great deal of the Indians, from observing them even in this broken and degraded condition. There is a language of eye and motion which cannot be put into words, and which teaches what words never can. I feel acquainted with the soul of this race; I read its nobler thought in their defaced figures. There ***was*** a greatness, unique and precious, which he who does not feel will never duly appreciate the majesty of nature in this American continent.

I have mentioned that the Indian orator, who addressed the agents on this occasion, said, the difference between the white man and the red man is this: "the white man no sooner came here, than he thought of preparing the way for his posterity; the red man never thought of this." I was assured this was exactly his phrase; and it defines the true difference. We get the better because we do

"Look before and after."

But, from the same cause, we

"Pine for what is not."

The red man, when happy, was thoroughly happy; when good, was simply good. He needed the medal, to let him know that he ***was*** good.

These evenings we were happy, looking over the old-fashioned garden, over the beach, over the waters and pretty island opposite, beneath the growing moon; we did not stay to see it full at Mackinaw. At two o'clock, one night, or rather morning, the Great Western came snorting in, and we must go; and Mackinaw, and all the north-west summer, is now to me no more than picture and dream;--

"A dream within a dream."

These last days at Mackinaw have been pleasanter than the "lonesome" nine, for I have recovered the companion with whom I set out from the East, one who sees all, prizes all, enjoys much, interrupts never.

At Detroit we stopped for half a day. This place is famous in our history, and the unjust anger at its surrender is still expressed by almost every one who passes there. I had always shared the common feeling on this subject; for the indignation at a disgrace to our arms that seemed so unnecessary, has been handed down from father to child, and few of us have taken the pains to ascertain where the blame lay. But now, upon the spot, having read all the testimony, I felt convinced that it should rest solely with the government, which, by neglecting to sustain General Hull, as he had a right to expect they would, compelled him to take this step, or sacrifice many lives, and of the defenceless inhabitants, not of soldiers, to the cruelty of a savage foe, for the sake of his reputation.

I am a woman, and unlearned in such affairs; but, to a person with common sense and good eyesight, it is clear, when viewing the location, that, under the circumstances, he had no prospect of successful defence, and that to attempt it would have been an act of vanity, not valor.

I feel that I am not biased in this judgment by my personal relations, for I have always heard both sides, and, though my feelings had been moved by the picture of the old man sitting down, in the midst of his children, to a retired and despoiled old age, after a life of honor and happy intercourse with the public, yet tranquil, always secure that justice must be done at last, I supposed, like others, that he deceived himself, and deserved to pay the penalty for failure to the responsibility he had undertaken. Now on the spot, I change, and believe the country at large must, ere long, change from this opinion. And I wish to add my testimony, however trifling its weight, before it be drowned in the voice of general assent, that I may do some justice to the feelings which possessed me here and now.

A noble boat, the Wisconsin, was to be launched this afternoon, the whole town was out in many-colored array, the band playing. Our boat swept round to a good position, and all was ready but--the Wisconsin, which could not be made to stir. This was quite a disappointment. It would have been an imposing sight.

In the boat many signs admonished that we were floating eastward. A shabbily dressed phrenologist laid his hand on every head which would bend, with half-conceited, half-sheepish expression, to the trial of his skill. Knots of people gathered here and there to discuss points of theology. A bereaved lover was seeking religious consolation in--Butler's Analogy, which he had purchased for that purpose. However, he did not turn over many pages before his attention was drawn aside by the gay glances of certain damsels that came on board at Detroit, and, though Butler might afterwards be seen sticking from his pocket, it had not weight to impede him from many a feat of lightness and liveliness. I doubt if it went with him from the boat. Some there were, even, discussing the doctrines of Fourier. It seemed pity they were not going to, rather than from, the rich and free country where it would be so much easier, than with us, to try the great experiment of voluntary association, and show, beyond a doubt, that "an ounce of prevention is worth a pound of cure," a maxim of the "wisdom of nations," which has proved of little practical efficacy as yet.

Better to stop before landing at Buffalo, while I have yet the advantage over some of my readers.

* * * * *

THE BOOK TO THE READER

WHO OPENS, AS AMERICAN READERS OFTEN DO, AT THE END,
WITH DOGGEREL SUBMISSION.

To see your cousin in her country home,
If at the time of blackberries you come,
"Welcome, my friends," she cries with ready glee,
"The fruit is ripened, and the paths are free.
But, madam, you will tear that handsome gown;
The little boy be sure to tumble down;
And, in the thickets where they ripen best,
The matted ivy, too, its bower has drest.
And then, the thorns your hands are sure to rend,
Unless with heavy gloves you will defend;
Amid most thorns the sweetest roses blow,
Amid most thorns the sweetest berries grow."

If, undeterred, you to the fields must go,
  You tear your dresses and you scratch your hands;
But, in the places where the berries grow,
  A sweeter fruit the ready sense commands,
Of wild, gay feelings, fancies springing sweet--

Of bird-like pleasures, fluttering and fleet.

Another year, you cannot go yourself,
  To win the berries from the thickets wild,
And housewife skill, instead, has filled the shelf
  With blackberry jam, "by best receipts compiled,--
Not made with country sugar, for too strong
The flavors that to maple juice belong;
But foreign sugar, nicely mixed 'to suit
The taste,' spoils not the fragrance of the fruit."

"'Tis pretty good," half-tasting, you reply,
"I scarce should know it from fresh blackberry.
But the best pleasure such a fruit can yield,
Is to be gathered in the open field;
If only as an article of food,
Cherry or crab-apple are quite as good;
And, for occasions of festivity,
West India sweetmeats you had better buy."

Thus, such a dish of homely sweets as these
In neither way may chance the taste to please.

Yet try a little with the evening-bread;
Bring a good needle for the spool of thread;
Take fact with fiction, silver with the lead,
And, at the mint, you can get gold instead;
In fine, read me, even as you would be read.

www.bookjungle.com *email: sales@bookjungle.com fax: 630-214-0564 mail: Book Jungle PO Box 2226 Champaign, IL 61825*

The Codes Of Hammurabi And Moses
W. W. Davies

QTY

The discovery of the Hammurabi Code is one of the greatest achievements of archaeology, and is of paramount interest, not only to the student of the Bible, but also to all those interested in ancient history...

Religion   **ISBN:** *1-59462-338-4*   Pages:132
MSRP $12.95

The Theory of Moral Sentiments
Adam Smith

QTY

This work from 1749. contains original theories of conscience amd moral judgment and it is the foundation for systemof morals.

Philosophy   **ISBN:** *1-59462-777-0*   Pages:536
MSRP $19.95

Jessica's First Prayer
Hesba Stretton

QTY

In a screened and secluded corner of one of the many railway-bridges which span the streets of London there could be seen a few years ago, from five o'clock every morning until half past eight, a tidily set-out coffee-stall, consisting of a trestle and board, upon which stood two large tin cans, with a small fire of charcoal burning under each so as to keep the coffee boiling during the early hours of the morning when the work-people were thronging into the city on their way to their daily toil...

Childrens   **ISBN:** *1-59462-373-2*   Pages:84
MSRP $9.95

My Life and Work
Henry Ford

QTY

Henry Ford revolutionized the world with his implementation of mass production for the Model T automobile. Gain valuable business insight into his life and work with his own auto-biography... "We have only started on our development of our country we have not as yet, with all our talk of wonderful progress, done more than scratch the surface. The progress has been wonderful enough but..."

Biographies/   **ISBN:** *1-59462-198-5*   Pages:300
MSRP $21.95

www.bookjungle.com email: sales@bookjungle.com fax: 630-214-0564 mail: Book Jungle PO Box 2226 Champaign, IL 61825

The Art of Cross-Examination
Francis Wellman

QTY

I presume it is the experience of every author, after his first book is published upon an important subject, to be almost overwhelmed with a wealth of ideas and illustrations which could readily have been included in his book, and which to his own mind, at least, seem to make a second edition inevitable. Such certainly was the case with me; and when the first edition had reached its sixth impression in five months, I rejoiced to learn that it seemed to my publishers that the book had met with a sufficiently favorable reception to justify a second and considerably enlarged edition. ..

Reference   ISBN: *1-59462-647-2*   Pages:412   MSRP *$19.95*

On the Duty of Civil Disobedience
Henry David Thoreau

QTY

Thoreau wrote his famous essay, On the Duty of Civil Disobedience, as a protest against an unjust but popular war and the immoral but popular institution of slave-owning. He did more than write—he declined to pay his taxes, and was hauled off to gaol in consequence. Who can say how much this refusal of his hastened the end of the war and of slavery ?

Law   ISBN: *1-59462-747-9*   Pages:48   MSRP *$7.45*

Dream Psychology Psychoanalysis for Beginners
Sigmund Freud

QTY

Sigmund Freud, born Sigismund Schlomo Freud (May 6, 1856 - September 23, 1939), was a Jewish-Austrian neurologist and psychiatrist who co-founded the psychoanalytic school of psychology. Freud is best known for his theories of the unconscious mind, especially involving the mechanism of repression; his redefinition of sexual desire as mobile and directed towards a wide variety of objects; and his therapeutic techniques, especially his understanding of transference in the therapeutic relationship and the presumed value of dreams as sources of insight into unconscious desires.

Psychology   ISBN: *1-59462-905-6*   Pages:196   MSRP *$15.45*

The Miracle of Right Thought
Orison Swett Marden

QTY

Believe with all of your heart that you will do what you were made to do. When the mind has once formed the habit of holding cheerful, happy, prosperous pictures, it will not be easy to form the opposite habit. It does not matter how improbable or how far away this realization may see, or how dark the prospects may be, if we visualize them as best we can, as vividly as possible, hold tenaciously to them and vigorously struggle to attain them, they will gradually become actualized, realized in the life. But a desire, a longing without endeavor, a yearning abandoned or held indifferently will vanish without realization.

Self Help   ISBN: *1-59462-644-8*   Pages:360   MSRP *$25.45*

www.bookjungle.com *email: sales@bookjungle.com fax: 630-214-0564 mail: Book Jungle PO Box 2226 Champaign, IL 61825*

QTY

☐ **The Rosicrucian Cosmo-Conception Mystic Christianity** by **Max Heindel**   ISBN: *1-59462-188-8*   **$38.95**
The Rosicrucian Cosmo-conception is not dogmatic, neither does it appeal to any other authority than the reason of the student. It is: not controversial, but is: sent forth in the, hope that it may help to clear...   New Age/Religion Pages 646

☐ **Abandonment To Divine Providence** by **Jean-Pierre de Caussade**   ISBN: *1-59462-228-0*   **$25.95**
"The Rev. Jean Pierre de Caussade was one of the most remarkable spiritual writers of the Society of Jesus in France in the 18th Century. His death took place at Toulouse in 1751. His works have gone through many editions and have been republished...   Inspirational/Religion Pages 400

☐ **Mental Chemistry** by **Charles Haanel**   ISBN: *1-59462-192-6*   **$23.95**
Mental Chemistry allows the change of material conditions by combining and appropriately utilizing the power of the mind. Much like applied chemistry creates something new and unique out of careful combinations of chemicals the mastery of mental chemistry...   New Age Pages 354

☐ **The Letters of Robert Browning and Elizabeth Barret Barrett 1845-1846 vol II**   ISBN: *1-59462-193-4*   **$35.95**
by **Robert Browning** and **Elizabeth Barrett**   Biographies Pages 596

☐ **Gleanings In Genesis (volume I)** by **Arthur W. Pink**   ISBN: *1-59462-130-6*   **$27.45**
Appropriately has Genesis been termed "the seed plot of the Bible" for in it we have, in germ form, almost all of the great doctrines which are afterwards fully developed in the books of Scripture which follow...   Religion/Inspirational Pages 420

☐ **The Master Key** by **L. W. de Laurence**   ISBN: *1-59462-001-6*   **$30.95**
In no branch of human knowledge has there been a more lively increase of the spirit of research during the past few years than in the study of Psychology, Concentration and Mental Discipline. The requests for authentic lessons in Thought Control, Mental Discipline and...   New Age/Business Pages 422

☐ **The Lesser Key Of Solomon Goetia** by **L. W. de Laurence**   ISBN: *1-59462-092-X*   **$9.95**
This translation of the first book of the "Lernegton" which is now for the first time made accessible to students of Talismanic Magic was done, after careful collation and edition, from numerous Ancient Manuscripts in Hebrew, Latin, and French...   New Age/Occult Pages 92

☐ **Rubaiyat Of Omar Khayyam** by **Edward Fitzgerald**   ISBN: *1-59462-332-5*   **$13.95**
Edward Fitzgerald, whom the world has already learned, in spite of his own efforts to remain within the shadow of anonymity, to look upon as one of the rarest poets of the century, was born at Bredfield, in Suffolk, on the 31st of March, 1809. He was the third son of John Purcell...   Music Pages 172

☐ **Ancient Law** by **Henry Maine**   ISBN: *1-59462-128-4*   **$29.95**
The chief object of the following pages is to indicate some of the earliest ideas of mankind, as they are reflected in Ancient Law, and to point out the relation of those ideas to modern thought.   Religiom/History Pages 452

☐ **Far-Away Stories** by **William J. Locke**   ISBN: *1-59462-129-2*   **$19.45**
"Good wine needs no bush, but a collection of mixed vintages does. And this book is just such a collection. Some of the stories I do not want to remain buried for ever in the museum files of dead magazine-numbers an author's not unpardonable vanity..."   Fiction Pages 272

☐ **Life of David Crockett** by **David Crockett**   ISBN: *1-59462-250-7*   **$27.45**
"Colonel David Crockett was one of the most remarkable men of the times in which he lived. Born in humble life, but gifted with a strong will, an indomitable courage, and unremitting perseverance...   Biographies/New Age Pages 424

☐ **Lip-Reading** by **Edward Nitchie**   ISBN: *1-59462-206-X*   **$25.95**
Edward B. Nitchie, founder of the New York School for the Hard of Hearing, now the Nitchie School of Lip-Reading, Inc, wrote "LIP-READING Principles and Practice". The development and perfecting of this meritorious work on lip-reading was an undertaking...   How-to Pages 400

☐ **A Handbook of Suggestive Therapeutics, Applied Hypnotism, Psychic Science**   ISBN: *1-59462-214-0*   **$24.95**
by **Henry Munro**   Health/New Age/Health/Self-help Pages 376

☐ **A Doll's House: and Two Other Plays** by **Henrik Ibsen**   ISBN: *1-59462-112-8*   **$19.95**
Henrik Ibsen created this classic when in revolutionary 1848 Rome. Introducing some striking concepts in playwriting for the realist genre, this play has been studied the world over.   Fiction/Classics/Plays 308

☐ **The Light of Asia** by **sir Edwin Arnold**   ISBN: *1-59462-204-3*   **$13.95**
In this poetic masterpiece, Edwin Arnold describes the life and teachings of Buddha. The man who was to become known as Buddha to the world was born as Prince Gautama of India but he rejected the worldly riches and abandoned the reigns of power when...   Religion/History/Biographies Pages 170

☐ **The Complete Works of Guy de Maupassant** by **Guy de Maupassant**   ISBN: *1-59462-157-8*   **$16.95**
"For days and days, nights and nights, I had dreamed of that first kiss which was to consecrate our engagement, and I knew not on what spot I should put my lips..."   Fiction/Classics Pages 240

☐ **The Art of Cross-Examination** by **Francis L. Wellman**   ISBN: *1-59462-309-0*   **$26.95**
Written by a renowned trial lawyer, Wellman imparts his experience and uses case studies to explain how to use psychology to extract desired information through questioning.   How-to/Science/Reference Pages 408

☐ **Answered or Unanswered?** by **Louisa Vaughan**   ISBN: *1-59462-248-5*   **$10.95**
Miracles of Faith in China   Religion Pages 112

☐ **The Edinburgh Lectures on Mental Science (1909)** by **Thomas**   ISBN: *1-59462-008-3*   **$11.95**
This book contains the substance of a course of lectures recently given by the writer in the Queen Street Hall, Edinburgh. Its purpose is to indicate the Natural Principles governing the relation between Mental Action and Material Conditions...   New Age/Psychology Pages 148

☐ **Ayesha** by **H. Rider Haggard**   ISBN: *1-59462-301-5*   **$24.95**
Verily and indeed it is the unexpected that happens! Probably if there was one person upon the earth from whom the Editor of this, and of a certain previous history, did not expect to hear again...   Classics Pages 380

☐ **Ayala's Angel** by **Anthony Trollope**   ISBN: *1-59462-352-X*   **$29.95**
The two girls were both pretty, but Lucy who was twenty-one who supposed to be simple and comparatively unattractive, whereas Ayala was credited, as her Bombwhat romantic name might show, with poetic charm and a taste for romance. Ayala when her father died was nineteen...   Fiction Pages 484

☐ **The American Commonwealth** by **James Bryce**   ISBN: *1-59462-286-8*   **$34.45**
An interpretation of American democratic political theory. It examines political mechanics and society from the perspective of Scotsman James Bryce   Politics Pages 572

☐ **Stories of the Pilgrims** by **Margaret P. Pumphrey**   ISBN: *1-59462-116-0*   **$17.95**
This book explores pilgrims religious oppression in England as well as their escape to Holland and eventual crossing to America on the Mayflower, and their early days in New England...   History Pages 268

www.bookjungle.com *email:* sales@bookjungle.com *fax:* 630-214-0564 *mail:* Book Jungle PO Box 2226 Champaign, IL 61825

QTY

The Fasting Cure *by Sinclair Upton* ISBN: *1-59462-222-1* **$13.95**
In the Cosmopolitan Magazine for May, 1910, and in the Contemporary Review (London) for April, 1910, I published an article dealing with my experiences in fasting. I have written a great many magazine articles, but never one which attracted so much attention... *New Age/Self Help/Health Pages 164*

Hebrew Astrology *by Sepharial* ISBN: *1-59462-308-2* **$13.45**
In these days of advanced thinking it is a matter of common observation that we have left many of the old landmarks behind and that we are now pressing forward to greater heights and to a wider horizon than that which represented the mind-content of our progenitors... *Astrology Pages 144*

Thought Vibration or The Law of Attraction in the Thought World ISBN: *1-59462-127-6* **$12.95**
by William Walker Atkinson *Psychology/Religion Pages 144*

Optimism *by Helen Keller* ISBN: *1-59462-108-X* **$15.95**
Helen Keller was blind, deaf, and mute since 19 months old, yet famously learned how to overcome these handicaps, communicate with the world, and spread her lectures promoting optimism. An inspiring read for everyone... *Biographies/Inspirational Pages 84*

Sara Crewe *by Frances Burnett* ISBN: *1-59462-360-0* **$9.45**
In the first place, Miss Minchin lived in London. Her home was a large, dull, tall one, in a large, dull square, where all the houses were alike, and all the sparrows were alike, and where all the door-knockers made the same heavy sound... *Childrens/Classic Pages 88*

The Autobiography of Benjamin Franklin *by Benjamin Franklin* ISBN: *1-59462-135-7* **$24.95**
The Autobiography of Benjamin Franklin has probably been more extensively read than any other American historical work, and no other book of its kind has had such ups and downs of fortune. Franklin lived for many years in England, where he was agent... *Biographies/History Pages 332*

Name	
Email	
Telephone	
Address	
City, State ZIP	

☐ Credit Card   ☐ Check / Money Order

Credit Card Number	
Expiration Date	
Signature	

Please Mail to: Book Jungle
PO Box 2226
Champaign, IL 61825
or Fax to: 630-214-0564

ORDERING INFORMATION

web: www.bookjungle.com
email: sales@bookjungle.com
fax: 630-214-0564
mail: Book Jungle PO Box 2226 Champaign, IL 61825
or PayPal to sales@bookjungle.com

Please contact us for bulk discounts

DIRECT-ORDER TERMS

20% Discount if You Order Two or More Books
Free Domestic Shipping!
Accepted: Master Card, Visa, Discover, American Express

www.ingramcontent.com/pod-product-compliance
Lightning Source LLC
Chambersburg PA
CBHW081231170426
43198CB00017B/2725